Barcelona Travel Guide 2023 & Beyond

The Ultimate Handbook for First-Time Visitors and Seasoning Travelers to Barcelona

Alexander J Collins

Copyright

Except for brief quotations incorporated in critical reviews and certain other noncommercial uses permitted by copyright law, no part of this publication may be reproduced, distributed, or transmitted in any form or by any means, including photocopying, recording, or other electronic or mechanical methods, without the publisher's prior written permission.

Barcelona Travel Guide 2023 & Beyond: The Ultimate Handbook for First-Time Visitors and Seasoning Travelers to Barcelona

All rights reserved.

Copyright ©2023 Alexander J Collins

Overview...**6**

Chapter 1: Introduction to Barcelona **8**

> **Brief History of Barcelona** **9**
>> Foundation and Medieval growth...9
>> The modern city 11
>> Barcelona Province 12
>
> **An overview of the city and its neighborhoods**................**14**
>
> **Planning Your Trip to Barcelona** **17**

Chapter 2: Accommodation in Barcelona **22**

> **The Best ten luxury hotels in Barcelona**...........................**24**
>
> **The 12 best low-budget hotels in Barcelona** **37**

Chapter 3: Top Attractions in Barcelona........................**46**

> **Exploring the Gothic Quarter** **49**
>
> **Visiting the Sagrada Familia** **52**
>
> **Discovering The Park Guell** **55**
>
> **Exploring the La Rambla** **58**
>
> **Visiting The Picasso Museum** **61**
>
> **The Camp Nou**..**63**
>
> **Exploring Casa Batllo** **66**

The La Boqueria Market 69

Discovery The Magic Fountain of Montjuic 72

Visiting The Tibidabo 74

Enjoying the Beaches of Barcelona 76

    Barceloneta Beach 77

    Nova Icaria Beach 80

    Bogatell Beach 81

    Sant Sebastia Beach 83

Chapter 4: Barcelona's Food and Drink Scene 86

    The best places to eat in Barcelona 88

Chapter 5: Shopping in Barcelona 94

    Passeig de Gracia 97

    La Roca Village 99

    El Corte Ingles 101

    Mercat de la Boqueria 103

    Portal de l'Angel 104

    Encants Vells 106

    Gracia Neighborhood 108

    Rambla de Catalunya 109

Chapter 6: Day Trips from Barcelona 112

    A Day trip to Montserrat 114

    A Day Trip to Sitges 116

    A Day trip to Girona 118

    A Day trip to Costa Brava 121

    A Day trip to Tarragona 123

Chapter 7: How to stay safe in Barcelona 126

    Security alerts 129

    Pickpockets Barcelona 131

    Ten quick Barcelona safety tips 132

    How to avoid being robbed in Barcelona 135

Over 100 common Spanish phrases with their translations 154

    The book summary 162

    Conclusion 164

    Reference 166

Barcelona Travel Guide 2023 & Beyond

The Ultimate Handbook for
First-Time Visitors and Seasoning Travelers
To Barcelona

Overview

Barcelona is a city with endless amenities. There is something for everyone in the Catalan city, from magnificent architecture and internationally famous art to delicious food and thriving nightlife. You could feel overburdened as a first-time tourist to Barcelona by the number of alternatives and attractions to see. This travel guidebook is available to assist you in making the most of your stay in Barcelona by helping you organize your trip.

The best guide for both first-time visitors and seasoned tourists to this stunning city is Barcelona Travel Guide 2023. This book has all the information you need to plan your Trip, such as when to go, how to get there, and where to stay.

Additionally, you'll learn about the top sights to see, the finest restaurants and bars, as well as the iconic sites and undiscovered secrets that define Barcelona.

This travel manual will assist you in navigating Barcelona like an expert, whether you're there for a single adventure, a family holiday, or a romantic break. You will feel comfortable and confident exploring the city, from the lively alleys of the Gothic Quarter to the Barceloneta charming beaches.

You'll find comprehensive details on everything from the ideal time to visit Barcelona to useful advice for utilizing the city's public transit system in the following chapters. You'll also get insider tips on where to buy, eat, and drink, as well as suggestions for day trips for those who want to explore the region.

In other words, Barcelona Travel Guide 2023 has got you covered whether you're a culture vulture, a foodie, or an adventure seeker. Let's get arranging for your ideal trip to Barcelona!

Chapter 1: Introduction to Barcelona

Catalonia is located in the northeastern part of Spain, and Barcelona serves as the region's capital city. It is the second-largest city in Spain after the capital Madrid, with a population that is greater than 1.6 million people. The city's proximity to the Mediterranean Sea, as well as its beaches, pleasant climate, and dynamic culture, all contributed to its status as a popular tourist destination.

The city of Barcelona has a long and illustrious past, which can be seen in the city's architecture, its art, and its traditions. Over two thousand years ago, the Romans established the city, and the historic Gothic Quarter of the city still maintains traces of its long and illustrious history. Barcelona saw a cultural rebirth in the latter half of the 19th century and the early 20th century, during which time renowned painters such as Antoni Gaudi and Pablo Picasso made the city their permanent residence.

Nowadays, Barcelona is famous all over the world for its exciting nightlife, museums of international caliber, and breathtaking architecture. The city is a home to a very large number of well-known landmarks, some of which are the Gothic Quarter, the Sagrada Familia, and Park Guell. It is also a center for shopping, dining, and entertainment, with a dizzying array of restaurants, pubs, and clubs from which to pick.

Brief History of Barcelona

Foundation and Medieval growth

Tradition says that the Phoenicians or the Carthaginians, who had trade posts along the Catalonian coast, founded Barcelona. But people no longer think that the city got its name from the family of the leader of the Carthaginians, Hamilcar Barca. The Colonia Faventia Julia Augusta Pia Barcino was not a significant location during the Roman era.

Until the 3rd century CE. During the three hundred years that the Visigoths lived there, the city was called Barcinona. Before the Moors came in 717 CE, it became a very important sacred center.

The city, which the Moors called Barjelnah, was a top priority for the Carolingian Franks. They took control of it in 801, and the Ebro River on the border of Catalonia became the southern limit of their power. In 985, the forces of al-Manr, the top minister of the Umayyad caliphate of Córdoba, destroyed the city. In the 10th and 11th centuries, the Counts of Barcelona strengthened their control over Catalonia. After Catalonia and Aragon joined together in 1137, Barcelona grew into a major trade city.

In the 14th century, plague attacks hurt Barcelona, and when Naples became the capital of the Catalan-Aragonese kingdom in 1442, the city started to fall apart. The rise of the Habsburg Empire, the growing power of the Turks in the Mediterranean, and the discovery of America all made this decline worse. During the 17th century, things got worse with the court in Madrid. During the War of the Spanish Succession, Philip V of Spain attacked Barcelona after the Catalans let Archduke Charles III of Austria set up his court in Barcelona in 1705. This was to support his claim to the Spanish throne. After the city fell in 1714, Philip took away all of the ways that people could run their own affairs. In a strange way, this led to a time of wealth, which was helped a lot by the growth of the cotton industry.

The modern city

From 1808 to 1813, Barcelona was again occupied, this time by Napoleon's men. During the war with the French, the province was destroyed, but after the war, manufacturing began. Catalonia became Spain's wealthiest area after the textile industry grew. It also led to a fast rise in the number of people living there and to tensions between the bourgeoisie and industrial workers. Anarchist groups grew, and there was trouble all the way up to the Spanish Civil War. Notable events include the uprising of 1835, in which a number of convents were burned, the riots in the mid-1850s over the introduction of automatic machinery, and the Setmana Tràgica (Catalan for "Tragic Week") in 1909, which led to more church burning.

On the bright side, there were 400,000 people at the 1888 show, and by 1900, almost half of Spain's imports came through Catalonia. Due to the area's strong economy, calls for self-government grew again, and from 1913 to 1923, the area had some authority. In 1931, Barcelona became the capital of the Catalan Republic. The area got a lot of control over itself the next year, and when the Civil War broke out in 1936, it was the main center of Republican strength. When it fell in January 1939, the Republic finally gave up.

When Catalonia lost, it lost many rights and benefits, and for a while, it wasn't even allowed to speak Catalan. The Generalitat, which is an independent Catalan government, was only brought back in 1977. In 1979, Barcelona signed agreements with the national government of Spain that set up new places for self-government and encouraged a wide range of changes.

In 1992, Barcelona held the Olympics, which helped the city get back on its feet. The once-dilapidated waterfront was turned into a promenade, marina, restaurants, beaches, and cultural attractions. In the east of the city, a convention center and auditorium were built so that Forum 2004, an international gathering about economic growth and cultural diversity, could be held there.

Barcelona Province

Barcelona is a province in northeastern Spain. It is part of the autonomous community of Catalonia. It started out in 1833. The Llobregat River basin is the center of the province, and its areas are set up in a symmetrical way around it. No province has a more varied scenery than Catalonia. It is a cross-section of many different geological zones, The Pyrenees, the interior scarps and basins of Catalonia, the littoral ranges, the central depression, the coastal mountains, and the coastal plains are only a few examples.

As diverse as the land is, so is the business. Near Berga, in the mountainous northern tableland, lignite is mined, and the province is one of Spain's biggest makers of cement. Since Roman times, salt has been mined in the Cardona Valley in the southwest, and in 1912, potash reserves near Suria were found to be very large. Grapes grow in the fertile lands around Vic, Barcelona, and Villafranca in the south. All over the center depression, grains are grown. Around the Llobregat River valley, there is a lot of farming on the coastal plain. Because the province has a mild temperature, Mediterranean beaches, and cultural venues, tourism is a major source of income.

Barcelona can be described as one of the best places to make things in Spain, and Barcelona City, the local capital, is also the main seaport. More than three-quarters of all textile, paper, and plastic products are made in the city, and a lot of chemicals, cars, and tech are also made there. There are table wines, sparkling wines, and manufactured things that are exported. The province has made good use of its position and the hydroelectric power sources in the Pyrenees. From Barcelona city to Madrid city, there is a fast train. In the province, there is an airport. Area 2,984 square miles (7,728 square km). Pop. (2011) 5,522,566.

An overview of the city and its neighborhoods

The city of Barcelona is incredibly dynamic and diversified, and it contains a great number of various neighborhoods, each of which has its own unique personality and allure. There are ten different districts in the city, each of which is further subdivided into several different neighborhoods.

The Gothic Quarter, often known as the Barri Gotic, is the most well-known neighborhood in Barcelona. It is situated in the heart of the city's historic district. This neighborhood is home to some of the oldest structures and sites in all of Barcelona, such as the Cathedral of Barcelona, the Placa del Rei, and the Palau de la Generalitat. In addition to its name, the Gothic Quarter is famous for the small, twisting lanes and exquisite medieval architecture that can be found there.

El Raval is yet another well-liked area in Barcelona. This part of the city is famous for its artsy atmosphere and hipster atmosphere. In addition to being home to a number of chic cafes, bars, and stores, El Raval is also the location of the MACBA modern art museum. The neighborhood is also well-known for its multiethnic population, as many people who immigrated from countries in South Asia and North Africa made the area their home.

Another well-liked district in Barcelona is the Gracia neighborhood, which has a reputation for having a bohemian vibe and a more village-like environment. Gracia is home to a number of smaller plazas, sometimes known as squares, in which inhabitants congregate to chat and enjoy cafes with outdoor seating. The area is particularly well-known for its street festivals, the most well-known of which is the Festa Major de Gracia, which takes place on the first Sunday of every August.

Eixample, which is noted for its modernist architecture and designer stores, and Barceloneta, which is the city's seaside zone, are both prominent neighborhoods in Barcelona. Eixample is one of the most well-known neighborhoods in Barcelona. In addition, the neighborhoods of Sant Antoni,

Poble Nou, and Sants are well-liked by both natives of the city and tourists that come to visit.

Barcelona has a history and culture that is both rich and diverse, and this is reflected in the city's art, architecture, and traditions. The city has been inhabited since Roman times, and many of its most well-known buildings, including the Gothic Quarter and the Cathedral of Barcelona, date back to the medieval period. The city was named for the Gothic Quarter, which is located in the city.

Barcelona saw a cultural rebirth in the latter half of the 19th century and the early 20th century, during which time renowned painters such as Antoni Gaudi and Pablo Picasso made the city their permanent residence. The city is filled with examples of Gaudi's own brand of modernist architecture, the most well-known of which are the Sagrada Familia and Park Guell.

Today, Barcelona is well-known for having a global atmosphere and a culture that is alive and well. Throughout the course of the year, the city plays host to a wide variety of cultural events and festivals, the most notable of which are the La Mercè Festival in September and the Primavera Sound music festival in June. The city is also known as a center for modern art and design, and it contains a large number of galleries and museums that display examples of the most recent fashions and tendencies.

Planning Your Trip to Barcelona

If you are thinking about going to Barcelona, there are a few things that you need to keep in mind in order to make sure that your time there is relaxing and enjoyable without any hassles.

When to go: Barcelona is a popular destination all throughout the year, but the best time to visit is either between the months of May and June or between the months of September and November, when the weather is moderate, and the crowds are thinner.

Getting there is simple, as Barcelona not only has a sizable international airport, but it is also very well connected to the rest of the major cities in Europe by both train and bus.

Barcelona is home to a diverse selection of lodging alternatives, ranging from low-cost hostels to five-star hotels for the utmost comfort. It is highly recommended that you book your accommodations in advance, especially during the busiest times of the year for tourism.

Transit: Buses, metro trains, and trams are just some of the options available to passengers in Barcelona's well-developed public transit system. Investing in a T10 ticket, which permits the holder to take ten trips on any public transportation system and may be purchased at a reduced price, is a smart move to make.

The Sagrada Familia, Park Guell, and the Gothic Quarter are just a few of the must-see attractions that can be found in Barcelona, a city that is known for its various tourist attractions. Because waiting in line for popular attractions can be time-consuming, it is recommended that tickets be purchased in advance.

Food and drink: Barcelona is well-known for the high quality of its cuisine and wine; therefore, it is imperative that you try some of the regional delicacies, such as paella, tapas, and cava. You should also give some of the locally brewed craft beer a shot, as this style of beer, which has seen a surge in popularity in recent years.

Safety: Barcelona is a safe city; nonetheless, as in any other major city, it is vital to be aware of your surroundings and take precautions against pickpocketing and other forms of small crime.

You can make your vacation to Barcelona an experience that is not only memorable but also delightful by keeping these ideas in mind while you are there.

Getting to Barcelona

The city of Barcelona is a favorite vacation spot for people from all over the world since it is simple to reach.

By Air:

El Prat Airport (BCN), Barcelona's major international airport, is located about 14 kilometers (km) southwest of the city center and serves a wide range of destinations. The airport is served by major airlines from all over the world and provides daily direct flights to a large number of destinations located in Europe, North America, South America, Africa, and Asia. To get into the heart of the city from the airport, you can either take a cab, a bus, or a train.

By Train: Another convenient way to reach other major cities in Europe is by train, with trains arriving at Barcelona Sants station as well as Barcelona Estacio de Franca station. The city is easily accessible via high-speed trains from Paris, Marseille, and Lyon, as well as other towns in France. Additionally, the city is easily accessible via regional and high-speed trains from Madrid, Valencia, and other cities in Spain.

By Bus: Another convenient method of transportation to get to Barcelona is by bus. Many national and international bus companies, like Eurolines and Flixbus, provide services to and from the city. Since the bus terminal in Barcelona is situated in the middle of the city, it will not be difficult for you to go to your lodging.

By Car:

If you'd rather travel by car, Barcelona is conveniently connected to other major cities in Spain, like Madrid and Valencia, by a network of motorways. However, due to the fact that traffic in the city center may become quite congested, it is typically simpler to make use of Barcelona's public transit once you have arrived in the city.

It doesn't matter where you're coming from—Barcelona is reachable via a wide variety of transport modes, which is one reason why this city is such a popular travel destination among tourists from all over the world.

Barcelona Travel Guide 2023 & Beyond

Chapter 2: Accommodation in Barcelona

From five-star hotels to low-cost hostels, Barcelona provides visitors with a diverse selection of lodging alternatives to meet their individual needs, preferences, and budgets.

Hotels: If you plan to stay in Barcelona, you will have a wide variety of hotel options to select from, ranging from opulent 5-star hotels to more wallet-friendly 2-star ones. The location of a hotel, the number of services it offers, and the season all have a significant impact on the cost of staying there. It is smart to do research on hotels in advance and compare their rates in order to get the most affordable option. You are able to make reservations for hotels by using intermediary websites like Booking.com and Expedia, as well as the individual hotel websites itself.

Hostels: Hostels are a popular alternative for visitors to Barcelona who are looking to keep their travel costs to a minimum. There are a large number of hostels located all over the city that provide both shared dorms and individual rooms for their guests. Online booking services such as Hostelworld, Booking.com, and Airbnb allow users to reserve stays in hostels across the world.

Apartments: If you want more room and solitude, renting an apartment may be a suitable alternative for you to consider. Apartments can be rented by the month or by the week. In Barcelona, there are a large number of apartments that are offered for short-term rentals. These flats range from simple studios to opulent penthouses. Apartments are available for rent on many internet booking sites, including Booking.com, Airbnb, and HomeAway, among others.

Price Range: The range of prices for lodging in Barcelona can change quite a bit based on the time of year and the location of the property. You should anticipate paying a higher rate for lodging if you choose to stay in the heart of the city or during the busiest time of the year for tourism. The cost of a night's stay in hostels or cheap hotels can range anywhere from 20 to 70 euros, while the cost of a night's stay at a hotel in the middle price range can be anywhere from 80 to 150 euros. The cost of a night's stay at a luxury hotel or apartment might easily exceed €200.

Before making a reservation, it is recommended to do some research on the available lodging options and compare the rates of these options with one another. If you want to save money on accommodations, you might also think about making reservations in advance or during the off-season.

The Best ten luxury hotels in Barcelona

It should come as no surprise that Barcelona, a city that oozes luxury and style, has a wide selection of hotels that fall into the luxury hotel category. It doesn't matter if you're in Barcelona for business or pleasure; if you stay at any one of these top 10 luxury hotels, your vacation will undoubtedly be one of the most memorable experiences of your life.

Hotel Arts Barcelona

One of the most famous and opulent hotels in all of Barcelona is the Hotel Arts Barcelona, which can be found at the Olympic Village on the water's edge. The hotel features five-star amenities such as a spa, a fitness center, and a restaurant that has earned a Michelin star, in addition to offering breathtaking views of the city skyline and the Mediterranean Sea. The correct address is Marina, 19-21, 08005 Barcelona, Spain. Phone: +34 932 21 10 00. The cost of a night's stay begins at €370.

Mandarin Oriental Barcelona

The Mandarin Oriental Barcelona can is found in the very center of the city, putting guests within easy walking distance of several of the city's most famous sights. The hotel offers luxurious accommodations, including rooms and suites, a rooftop patio with a pool, and a restaurant with a Michelin star. Address: Passeig de Gràcia, 38-40, 08007 Barcelona, Spain. Phone: +34 931 51 88 88. The cost of a night's stay starts at 470 euros.

The Serras

The Serras is a high-end boutique hotel that can be found in the hip and happening district of El Born. The hotel offers luxurious accommodations, including rooms and suites, a rooftop patio with a pool and breathtaking vistas of the city, and a restaurant that has earned a Michelin star. Passeig de Colom, number 9, 08002, Barcelona, Spain. Phone: +34 935 48 80 00. The cost of a night's stay starts at 320 euros.

Hotel Casa Fuster

The old structure that now houses the Hotel Casa Fuster can be found on the prestigious Passeig de Gràcia in Barcelona. It has been completely renovated into a five-star establishment. The hotel offers luxurious accommodations, including rooms and suites, a rooftop patio with a pool, and an upscale restaurant. Address: Passeig de Gràcia, 132, 08008 Barcelona, Spain. Phone: +34 932 55 30 00. The cost of a night's stay begins at €250.

Hotel Neri Relais & Châteaux

The Hotel Neri Relais & Chateaux is a five-star establishment that can be found in the Gothic Quarter of Barcelona. The hotel offers luxurious accommodations, including rooms and suites, a rooftop patio with a pool, and a restaurant with a Michelin star. Address: Carrer de Sant Sever, 5, 08002 Barcelona, Spain. Phone: +34 933 04 06 55. The cost of a night's stay begins at €290.

Ohla Barcelona

Ohla Barcelona is a premium boutique hotel featuring elegant rooms and suites, a rooftop patio with a pool, and a restaurant that has been awarded a Michelin star. It is situated in the historically significant neighborhood of Eixample. Address: Via Laietana, 49, 08003 Barcelona, Spain. Phone: +34 933 41 50 50. The cost of a night's stay begins at €250.

Majestic Hotel & Spa Barcelona GL

The Majestic Hotel & Spa Barcelona GL is a five-star establishment that boasts a prestigious location on the world-famous Passeig de Gràcia. The hotel offers luxurious accommodations, including rooms and suites, a rooftop patio with a pool, and a restaurant with a Michelin star. Address: Passeig de Gràcia, 68, 08007 Barcelona, Spain. Phone: +34 934 88 17 17. The cost of a night's stay begins at €350.

Alma Barcelona

In the middle of the Eixample neighborhood in Barcelona is where you'll find the opulent boutique hotel known as Alma Barcelona. The hotel enjoys a well-deserved reputation for being one of the most chic and refined lodging options available in Barcelona.

The gorgeous rooftop terrace of the Alma Barcelona Hotel, which has both a small swimming pool and a breathtaking view of the city, is one of the most notable aspects of the hotel. After a long day of exploring Barcelona's landmarks, you'll find that this is the ideal place to relax and unwind.

The rooms and suites of Alma Barcelona are elegantly designed, with a focus on comfortable luxury and understated elegance. In each of the rooms, you'll find luxurious linen, premium toiletries, and other contemporary conveniences like flat-screen TVs and complimentary Wi-Fi.

In addition, the hotel features a fine dining establishment known as the Alma Mater Restaurant, which presents a modern perspective on the traditional food of Catalonia. The restaurant has been singled out for praise by a number of critics and is regarded as one of the top eating establishments in Barcelona.

You can book a reservation at the Alma Barcelona by calling the hotel directly or sending an email to the hotel's reservation desk if you are interested in staying there. The location of the hotel is at Carrer de Mallorca 269, which is in the 08008 neighborhood of Barcelona, Spain. The number that you need to call is +34 933 80 70 00.

Because Alma Barcelona is a luxury hotel, you should be prepared to pay a higher rate for your room during your time there. The cost of a room starts at about €250 per night but can go up significantly depending on the room type, as well as the time of year. If, on the other hand, you want to stay in a place that is both opulent and chic while yet being located in the middle of Barcelona, Alma Barcelona is a great alternative to take into consideration.

Mandarin Oriental Barcelona

The Gothic Quarter of Barcelona is home to the opulent Mandarin Oriental Barcelona, which serves as the city's premier luxury hotel. The hotel features outstanding architecture and design, and it also incorporates a number of modern elements that combine to produce a posh and elegant ambiance.

The hotel's rooms and suites all come equipped with contemporary conveniences such as premium bedding, free wireless internet access, and flat-screen televisions. The hotel provides its guests with a variety of services and amenities, such as a fitness center, a spa, and a pool located on the hotel's rooftop.

Moments, the Michelin-starred restaurant at the Mandarin Oriental Barcelona, is one of the hotel's most notable attractions since it presents a contemporary interpretation of traditional Catalan cuisine. The eatery is well-liked by gourmands and is thought to be one of the best places to eat in the city.

You can book a reservation at the Mandarin Oriental Barcelona by calling the hotel directly or sending an email to the hotel's reservations desk if you are interested in staying there. The location of the hotel is at Passeig de Gràcia, 38-40, in the 08007 neighborhood of Barcelona, Spain. The number that you need to call is +34 931 51 88 88.

Standard accommodation rates at the Mandarin Oriental Barcelona begin at approximately €400 per night. These room rates are considered to be on the higher end of the pricing spectrum. Those who are searching for a high-end place to stay in Barcelona, however, will find that this hotel's opulent amenities and convenient location make it an excellent option.

W Barcelona

The W Barcelona is a premium hotel that can be found in the area of Barceloneta, which lies directly on the beach. The hotel is renowned for its sophisticated and contemporary architecture, which places a focus on luxury and comfort.

The hotel's rooms and suites boast contemporary conveniences such as free Wi-Fi and flat-screen televisions, in addition to its breathtaking vistas of the Mediterranean Sea. The hotel offers a variety of services, such as a fitness center, a rooftop pool, and a spa for guests to enjoy during their stay.

Eclipse, the rooftop bar at the W Barcelona, is one of the hotel's most notable attractions since it affords guests breathtaking vistas of both the city and the sea. The bar is a favorite gathering place for both natives and visitors to the area because it is a wonderful location to enjoy a drink while taking in the breathtaking scenery.

You may book a reservation at the W Barcelona by calling the hotel directly or sending an email to the hotel's reservation desk if you are interested in staying there. The hotel's address is Placa de la Rosa dels Vents, 1, Final Passeig de Joan de Borbó, 08039 Barcelona, Spain. The number that you need to call is +34 932 95 28 00.

The W Barcelona has some of the most expensive accommodation prices in the city, with the base rate for a basic room beginning at approximately €350 per night. If, in contrast, you are seeking a high-end place to stay in Barcelona, this hotel is an excellent option due to its prime location directly on the beach as well as its lavish amenities.

The 12 best low-budget hotels in Barcelona

Are you considering taking a trip to Barcelona with a limited amount of money? There is no reason to be concerned because the city is home to a vast selection of hotels that come in a variety of price points and have both pleasant and practical accommodations. The following is a list of our top 10 choices for the most affordable hotels in Barcelona:

1. Hostal Barcelona

The Hostal Barcelona is a hotel that offers reasonable rates and is conveniently situated in the Gothic Quarter of the city.

The rooms at this hotel are on the simpler side but nevertheless offer a comfortable stay thanks to amenities like free Wi-Fi, flat-screen TVs, and private bathrooms. A single room will cost you approximately €40 per night while you stay here.

Address: Carrer de la Boqueria, 23, 08002 Barcelona, Spain
Phone number: +34 933 17 71 01

2. Hotel Barbara

The Eixample district is home to the quaint and affordable Hotel Barbara, which boasts a convenient location. The hotel provides comfortable rooms that are equipped with free Wi-Fi and flat-screen TVs, in addition to a front desk that is open around the clock and a luggage storage area. The cost of a night in a single room begins at approximately 50 Euros.

Address: C/ Marques de Barbera, 22, 08001 Barcelona, Spain Phone number: +34 933 01 70 75

3. Pension Segre

The Pension Segre is a straightforward hotel that yet manages to provide a nice stay for guests in the Barceloneta district. The hotel provides its guests with basic rooms that include complimentary Wi-Fi and communal bathrooms, as well as a front desk that is open around the clock and a luggage storage area. The lowest available rate for a single room is approximately €35 per night.

Telephone number: +34 933 10 30 01 Address: C/ Simon Oller, 1, 08001 Barcelona, Spain

4. Hotel Lyon

The Hotel Lyon is an economically friendly hotel that is situated in the center of the Gothic Quarter of the city. The hotel has rooms that are basic but pleasant, and they all come equipped with free Wi-Fi and flat-screen TVs. Additionally, there is a front desk that is open around the clock and a luggage storage area. A single room will cost you approximately €40 per night while you stay here.

Telephone number: +34 933 19 10 48 Address: C/ General Castaos, 6, 08003 Barcelona, Spain

5. Hostal Radio

The comfortable and affordable Hostal Radio may be found in the Raval neighborhood of Barcelona. The hotel has rooms that are basic but pleasant, and they all come equipped with free Wi-Fi and flat-screen TVs. Additionally, there is a front desk that is open around the clock and a luggage storage area. The cost of a night in a single room begins at approximately 50 Euros.

Carrer de Sant Vicenc, 39, 08001 Barcelona, Spain Telephone: +34 933 01 87 52 Address: Carrer de Sant Vicenc, 39

6. Hotel Adagio

The Hotel Adagio is a hotel that is easy on the wallet and can be found in the Eixample neighborhood. The hotel has rooms that are basic but pleasant, and they all come equipped with free Wi-Fi and flat-screen TVs. Additionally, there is a front desk that is open around the clock and a luggage storage area. The cost of a night in a single room begins at approximately 50 Euros.

Telephone number: +34 934 51 43 53 Address: C/ Girona, 116, 08009 Barcelona, Spain

7. Hostal Sans

The district of Sants is home to the low-cost hotel known as Hostal Sans. The hotel provides its guests with basic rooms that include complimentary Wi-Fi and communal bathrooms, as well as a front desk that is open around the clock and a luggage storage area. The lowest available rate for a single room is approximately €30 per night.

Address: C/ de la Creu Coberta, 83, 08014 Barcelona, Spain
Phone number: +34 934 23 11 53

8. Hotel 1898

The Hotel 1898 is a budget-friendly hotel that doesn't skimp on style or comfort despite its central location on La Rambla. Modern furniture fills the rooms, and come equipped with all of the conveniences necessary to ensure a relaxing stay for guests. In addition to a fitness facility and a spa, this hotel features a rooftop pool and bar with breathtaking views of the city. The cost of a night's stay begins at €100.

Phone number: +34 935 529 552 Address: La Rambla, 109, 08002 Barcelona, Spain

9. Casa Kessler Barcelona

The Eixample neighborhood is home to the quaint and hospitable Casa Kessler Barcelona, a quaint and lovely boutique hotel. The rooms have a sophisticated aesthetic that is achieved through the use of original elements, high ceilings, and parquet flooring. In order to facilitate visitors' rest and relaxation, the hotel features a lounge area, a library, and a patio. The cost of a night's stay begins at €50.

Address: Carrer de Enric Granados, 30, 08008 Barcelona, Spain Phone: +34 934 51 25 70

10. Generator Hostel Barcelona

The Generator Hostel can be found in the Gracia region of Barcelona. It is a hip and fashionable hostel. The game room, a bar, a restaurant, and a rooftop terrace are some of the amenities offered by the hostel. Both the shared and individual accommodations are light and airy and up to date with all of today's conveniences. The cost of a night's stay begins at €20.

Address: Carrer de Còrsega, 373, 08037 Barcelona, Spain Phone: +34 932 20 02 85

11. Hotel Curiosity

The Gothic Quarter is home to the budget-friendly Hotel. The rooms are contemporary and comfortable, each including a flat-screen TV, complimentary wireless internet access, and air conditioning. The hotel provides a comfortable lounge space as well as a patio for guests to use when they want to unwind. The cost of a night's stay begins at €60.

Address: Carrer del Carme, 25, 08001 Barcelona, Spain
Phone: +34 933 02 28 52

12. Hotel Sagrada Familia

Hotel This hotel is conveniently positioned close to the world-famous Sagrada Familia Basilica and offers reasonable rates. The rooms are contemporary and comfortable, each including a flat-screen TV, complimentary wireless internet access, and air conditioning. The hotel features a bar as well as a patio that offers views of the surrounding city. The cost of a night's stay begins at €70.

Address: Carrer de Còrsega, 541, 08025 Barcelona, Spain
Phone: +34 932 32 11 88

Chapter 3: Top Attractions in Barcelona

Barcelona is a city that is full to the brim with breathtaking architecture, vibrant culture, and rich history. When you go to Barcelona, there are a few places that absolutely have to be on your itinerary, let's first highlight them before expanciating on each of the attraction:

Sagrada Familia: The Sagrada Familia is a sight in Barcelona that just cannot be missed. The towering chapel that Antoni Gaudi built is one of the city's most instantly recognizable attractions. There are guided walks for people who want to discover more about the building's history and architecture.

Park Guell: Another one of Gaudi's works of art, Park Guell is a fanciful park that is packed with brilliant mosaics, one-of-a-kind sculptures, and breathtaking vistas of the city. It is a wonderful spot to kick back, relax, and take in the splendor of Barcelona.

La Rambla: This well-known boulevard can be found right in the middle of Barcelona, and it is usually a hub of activity.

Due to the fact that it is lined with stores, cafes, and street performers, it is an excellent location at which to take in the vibrancy of the city.

Gothic Quarter: The Gothic Quarter, located in the city of Barcelona, is the historic hub of the city. It's a confusing labyrinth of winding alleyways, secret plazas, and ancient structures that date back to the time of the Romans. The numerous stores, cafes, and museums in the area are all open to the public for exploration.

Picasso Museum: The Picasso Museum has one of the largest collections of Picasso's art that can be found anywhere in the world. Visitors are able to view everything from the artist's first sketches to some of his most well-known works of art.

Camp Nou: Camp Nou, the stadium that serves as the home field for Barcelona's professional football team, FC Barcelona, is an essential destination for sports lovers. Visitors get the opportunity to take guided tours of the stadium, view the various trophies that have been won by the squad, and obtain information regarding the history of the club.

Casa Batllo: Gaudi's Casa Batllo is yet another one of the architect's architectural marvels. The one-of-a-kind structure is embellished with tiles of varying colors and forms, as well as a ceiling that undulates. Visitors get the opportunity to take a tour and gain insight into the thought process that went into the design.

La Boqueria Market: One of the oldest marketplaces in Barcelona is the Boqueria Market, also known as La Boqueria. It is a wonderful area to go shopping, whether you are looking for fresh veggies, meats, or seafood. In addition, guests have the opportunity to sample regional specialties such as Iberian ham and Spanish omelets.

The Magic Fountain of Montjuic: This magnificent fountain puts on a performance every evening with water, lights, and music to create an enchanted environment. It's a wonderful spot to wind down the day and take in the splendor of Barcelona once the sun goes down.

Tibidabo: The Tibidabo peak is a mountain that overlooks Barcelona and is home to a gorgeous church as well as an amusement park. Visitors can ride a cable car all the way to the summit of the mountain and take in breathtaking vistas of the city below.

These are only a few of the many sights and attractions that Barcelona, Spain, has to offer. In Barcelona, regardless matter whether you are interested in art, history, or simply soaking up the dynamic energy of the city, you will be able to find something that satisfies your needs. In the future, for the sake of greater comprehension, we are going to go deeper into each attraction.

Exploring the Gothic Quarter

The Gothic Quarter, which is sometimes referred to as the Barri Gotic, is Barcelona's oldest and most historically significant neighborhood. It is a labyrinth of little alleyways, secret squares, and ancient structures that date back to the time of the Romans and may be found in the central part of the city. Anyone who has an interest in architecture, history, or who simply wants to immerse themselves in the ambiance of old-world Europe needs to pay a visit to this region.

The Gothic Quarter is home to a number of important buildings and sites that are considered to be among the city's most popular tourist destinations. These include the Cathedral of Barcelona and the Placa del Rei. A magnificent specimen of Gothic architecture, the Cathedral of Barcelona, usually referred to as La Seu, can be found in Barcelona. It was constructed sometime between the 13th and 15th centuries and showcases a variety of architectural styles, such as Catalan Gothic and Baroque. Visitors who are interested in the building's history and architecture have the opportunity to take part in guided tours of the cathedral.

Placa del Rei, often referred to as the King's Square, is a stunning medieval square that was previously used as the residence of the Catalan monarchs. In medieval times, the area was known as the King's area. The area is encircled on all sides by historical structures, the most notable of which are the Palau Reial Major and the Chapel of St. Agatha. Visitors have the opportunity to take part in guided tours of the square, during which they may gain insight into its rich history and get a better look at the complex architecture.

In addition to its well-known landmarks, the Gothic Quarter is well-known for the winding lanes and hidden squares that can be found there. The Placa Reial, which is flanked on all sides by restaurants, cafes, and bars, is widely considered to be one of the most popular squares in the area. It's a nice area to get a drink and watch the world go by at the same time. Placa del Pi, Placa Sant Felip Neri, and Placa de Sant Jaume are a few of the city's other hidden squares that are well worth discovering.

In addition to the well-known sites and public spaces, the Gothic Quarter features a number of museums and art galleries for visitors to explore. Because it houses a collection of Pablo Picasso's works, the Picasso Museum is consistently ranked as one of the most visited museums in the region. The Frederic Mares Museum and the Barcelona History Museum are two further museums in the city that are well worth a visit.

Additionally famous for its retail establishments is the Gothic Quarter. The neighborhood is home to a number of stores that concentrate on handcrafted items such as jewelry, leather goods, and pottery, among other things. In addition, the region is home to a number of thrift stores and antique markets, both of which are accessible to tourists.

Anyone who goes to Barcelona should make it a point to stop by the Gothic Quarter at some point during their trip. This section of the city is one of a kind and sure to leave an impression thanks to its fascinating past, magnificent architecture, and charming hidden squares.

Visiting the Sagrada Familia

Sagrada Familia: A Masterpiece of Architecture and a Must-See Attraction in Barcelona

There is no doubt that the Sagrada Familia is one of the most well known landmarks in all of Barcelona, and with good reason. This magnificent basilica is the pinnacle of the labor that Catalan architect Antoni Gaudi did throughout his life. It is a masterpiece of Gothic and Art Nouveau architecture, and it is truly a sight to behold.

Gaudi took over as the primary architect of the Sagrada Familia in 1883, two years after construction of the church began in 1882. He worked on the project until the day he passed away in 1926, devoting the remainder of his life to its completion. Since that time, the basilica has been worked on by a number of different architects, and its construction has not been completed up to this day.

Visitors are welcome to come and see the Sagrada Familia, even though construction is still ongoing. It is a working Catholic church, and guests are welcome to join any of the services being held inside. But even if you don't practice any religion, you shouldn't miss the opportunity to see the basilica while you're in Barcelona.

The sheer magnitude of Sagrada Familia is one of the building's most arresting characteristics. The basilica is visible from a variety of different vantage points throughout the city due to its elevated position. The outside is elaborately carved with sculptures and carvings that reflect scenes from the Bible and the life of Jesus. The facade is detailed and beautiful.

However, the interior of the Sagrada Familia is where you'll find the true magic of the building. The inside was created by Gaudi to look like the interior of a forest, complete with towering columns that spread out like trees. The stained glass windows are quite stunning, and they project a rainbow of colors onto the walls and floor below them.

Visitors who love to find out more about the architecture and history of the Sagrada Familia can do so by taking a guided tour of the building. The trip grants visitors entrance to the museum, which features displays on the construction and design of the basilica, as well as the crypt, which is where Gaudi is interred after his death.

Tickets to the Sagrada Familia can be bought in advance through the Internet, which is highly recommended given the possibility of the attraction becoming overly crowded. The cost can change based on the kind of ticket you choose and whether or not you go on a guided tour.

In Barcelona, the Sagrada Familia is an attraction that you just cannot miss. The inventiveness and foresight of Antoni Gaudi are on full display here, and the result is a breathtaking site to witness in its own right. The basilica is bound to make an indelible mark on everybody who visits it, regardless of their religious beliefs.

Discovering The Park Guell

Park Guell: Exploring Gaudi's Whimsical Masterpiece in Barcelona

The extraordinary Park Guell may be found in the Gracia neighborhood of Barcelona. This park is one of a kind. The park is a whimsical wonderland that was designed by Antoni Gaudi, one of the most famous architects in the city. The park is filled with brilliant mosaics, one-of-a-kind sculptures, and breathtaking views over the city.

The project was supposed to be a housing development when it was started in the early 1900s, but it was eventually scrapped and converted into a public park instead. The park spans an area of 42 acres and is home to a variety of fascinating attractions, one of which is the well-known dragon monument located at the entrance.

The Sala Hipóstila is a vast room that is one of the most well-known features of the park. It is supported by 86 columns that come together to form a structure that resembles a forest. Mosaics of shattered ceramic tiles in vibrant colors adorn the room's ceiling, which is ornamented with the mosaics.

The Terrace of the Doric Order is yet another location that should not be missed because it provides breathtaking vistas of both the city and the Mediterranean Sea. The terrace is embellished with a variety of one-of-a-kind sculptures, such as the well-known lizard statue that has become an emblematic representation of the park.

In addition, guests have the opportunity to tour the Casa Museu Gaudi, the architect's former residence. In addition to displays focusing on Gaudi's life and career, the museum is home to a collection of the architect's personal things.

It is a wonderful location to unwind and take in the natural surroundings because, in addition to the various things to see and do in the park, there are also a number of hiking routes and picnic spots spread out over the park.

Travel Advice for the Park Guell Area:

- Purchase your tickets in advance to avoid waiting in huge lines at the entrance.
- Bring shoes that are comfortable for walking up and down hills, as the park has several of both.
- Always remember to bring a bottle of water and sunscreen with you, but this is especially important during the warmer months.
- If you want to see all of the key attractions in the park, you should plan to spend at least two hours there.
- Location: Carrer d'Olot, number s/n, 08024 Barcelona, Spain Contact information: +34 934 09 18 31
- The cost of admission is 10 Euros for each individual (as of the year 2023)
- The store is open from 8:30 in the morning until 8:00 at night from April to September, and then from 8:30 in the morning until 6:00 in the evening from October to March

Everyone who comes to Barcelona absolutely needs to make time to check out Park Guell. It's one of the most interesting and beautiful parks in the world, thanks to the one-of-a-kind combination of architecture, art, and nature that it features.

Take your time and enjoy all this beautiful park has to offer. By thoroughly exploring all of it.

Exploring the La Rambla

One of the most well-known avenues in Barcelona, La Rambla is also a well-liked destination for travelers who are in the city for business or pleasure. It begins from Placa de Catalunya and extends over a distance of 1.2 kilometers all the way to the Christopher Columbus Monument at Port Vell, which can be found in the very center of Barcelona. The following is an explanation of everything you need to know before going to La Rambla:

The history of La Rambla is both extensive and interesting. It dates back quite a ways. In the 14th century, it was a waterway that flowed outside the boundaries of the city where it is now located. In the course of time, it evolved into a bustling boulevard that served as a hub for social and cultural activities. It has evolved into a dynamic and busy boulevard that welcomes millions of tourists each and every year.

What to Do: There is a wide variety of things to do and sights to see along La Rambla. There are shops, restaurants, bars, and street performers at the both sides of the road.

You can take a stroll around the stalls at La Boqueria, which is one of the city's oldest markets, or you can go to the Gran Teatre del Liceu, which is a gorgeous opera venue that has been entertaining audiences since 1847.

Placa Reial is a gorgeous plaza that was constructed by Gaudi and is home to some of the most important structures in the city. If you are interested in history, you should make it a point to visit this area. You can also go to the Palau Guell, which is an impressive mansion that has been converted into a museum.

Where to Eat: La Rambla is well-known for its cuisine, and the neighborhood's many restaurants and cafes offer a diverse range of options. There are numerous restaurants, ranging from tapas bars to seafood restaurants, where you may indulge your sense of taste. Make it a point to sample some of the regional delicacies, such as paella, a rice meal that may be prepared with either seafood or pork and patatas bravas, a dish made up of hot tomato sauce and crunchy potatoes.

In the neighborhood of La Rambla, you may pick from a wide variety of hotels and youth hostels. You have the option of staying in hostels that are friendly to your wallet or Luxurious lodgings with spectacular city views. Hotel Royal Ramblas, Hotel Lloret Ramblas, and Hotel Pulitzer are just a few of the well-known establishments that can be found in close proximity to La Rambla.

La Rambla, like any other popular tourist location, can get very crowded, so it's crucial to watch out for pickpockets and keep your valuables close by. Keep your wallet and phone near to you at all times, and be aware that there may be pickpockets around. Additionally, it is recommended that you stay away from the street at night, especially if you are going by yourself.

Visiting The Picasso Museum

Visitors to Barcelona who have an interest in art should definitely make time to check out the Picasso Museum. One of the most well-known painters of the 20th century, Pablo Picasso, is honored here with a museum that celebrates both his life and his body of work. The museum is housed in five medieval palaces that are adjacent to one another and are located in the Gothic Quarter. These palaces were constructed in the 13th and 14th centuries. The collection is one of the largest collections of Picasso's works anywhere in the world because it contains more than 4,000 of the artist's pieces.

The museum is split up into a number of distinct parts, each of which is dedicated to a specific time period of Picasso's career. In the section titled Early Works, you'll find paintings, drawings, and sketches that Picasso created during his formative years when he was still experimenting with a variety of artistic styles and methods. Picasso struggled with melancholy and financial hardship throughout the time period covered by the Blue Period area of the museum. As a result, the artist produced a series of paintings in which various shades of blue predominate. The works that Picasso produced in the years that followed his Rose Period are colorful and upbeat, and the Rose Period section is loaded with them.

A lesser-known component of Picasso's body of work is represented in the museum by a collection of the artist's ceramics. These works illustrate Picasso's experimenting with shape and texture and demonstrate the whimsical side of his personality. The temporary exhibitions at the museum feature work by modern artists who have been affected by Picasso's work as well as works by other artists who were a member of Picasso's group of artists at the time.

Every other day of the week, including Mondays, the Picasso Museum is open to the public. The entrance charge is 12 euros; however, there are reductions available for students, senior citizens, and children under the age of 18. The museum provides docent-led tours in a variety of languages, including English, Spanish, and French, among others.

The Picasso Museum is one of the attractions in Barcelona that you won't want to skip if you're going to be there for any length of time. It doesn't matter if you consider yourself an art connoisseur or if you're just curious to find out more about one of the most well-known artists of all time; the museum's collection is certain to blow your mind. Because of its location in the Gothic Quarter, it is also an excellent starting point for excursions into the historic core of the city, and there are many shops, cafes, and restaurants in the immediate vicinity.

The Camp Nou

Camp Nou: The Ultimate Destination for Football Fans

If you are a fan of football, paying a visit to Camp Nou in Barcelona ought to be at the very top of your to-do list while you are there. This world-famous stadium is one of the most visited tourist attractions in the city, and it serves as the headquarters of the illustrious football club FC Barcelona. Everything you need to discover about Camp Nou is provided in the following.

An Overview of Camp Nou's Past

On September 24, 1957, FC Barcelona played a friendly match at Camp Nou against a group of players from the Spanish national team. This match served as the stadium's official opening. Since that time, the stadium has been the subject of a number of repairs and extensions, including the new grandstand's construction and the addition of additional seats to bring the total number of available seats up to 99,354. At the moment, it has the title of being the largest stadium in Europe and the third-largest stadium overall.

What to anticipate during your tour of Camp Nou

For any football fan visiting Barcelona, a visit to Camp Nou and a tour of the stadium is an absolute must. The stadium tour provides access to areas of the venue that are often off-limits to the general public and takes visitors behind the scenes of the stadium. You are welcome to tour the FC Barcelona museum as well as the team's locker rooms, the press room, the field, and even the pitch.

The museum houses a significant collection of memorabilia, which includes trophies, jerseys, and other historical relics. The collection is particularly outstanding. Visitors will have the opportunity to gain knowledge regarding the history of FC Barcelona and the club's most famous players, including Lionel Messi, Johan Cruyff, and Ronaldinho. In addition, there are interactive displays that give guests the opportunity to test their prowess on the football field and get a feel for what it would be like to play for the club.

The breathtaking vista that can be seen of the entire stadium when you reach the top of the grandstand is one of the highlights of the tour. The playing field, the city that surrounds it, and the well-known "Mes Que Un Club" (More Than a Club) sign can all be seen from this vantage point.

Travel advice for the Camp Nou stadium.

Wear comfortable shoes because there is a lot of walking involved in the trip.

If you are coming during the football season, try to attend a match at Camp Nou to experience the explosive atmosphere of a live game.

- Booking your tickets in advance will definitely help you avoid long lines at the stadium.
- Photography is permitted in the majority of locations of the stadium; however, the use of flash photography is not authorized.

Prices of tickets for the Camp Nou

Adult tickets for a tour of Camp Nou start at €26, while tickets for children younger than 13 years old cost €20. The price of admission grants visitors access to the museum as well as all other parts of the stadium that are part of the tour. Prices may change depending on the season as well as any unique events that are currently taking place.

Any football lover who is in Barcelona absolutely needs to make time to check out Camp Nou. The stadium is not only a remarkable accomplishment in terms of architecture, but it is also an essential monument in terms of the city's culture and history. Get ready to feel the excitement of Camp Nou by putting on the shirt of your favorite team, grabbing your camera, and getting set to go.

Exploring Casa Batllo

The Casa Batllo is one of the most well-known buildings designed by Antoni Gaudi and is an absolute must-see when in Barcelona. The building, which can be found in the middle of the city, has a characteristic facade, which helps it to stand out among the other structures that are located on the block.

The home was initially constructed in 1877, but in 1904, a wealthy textile merchant named Josep Batllo purchased the property and commissioned Gaudi to remodel it. Gaudi's work was completed in 1906. Gaudi undertook a comprehensive renovation of the structure, during which he incorporated the natural elements, vibrant colors, and organic contours that are characteristic of his work.

The building's facade is decorated in vibrant tiles, which are broken up by curving balconies and flowing lines that, depending on how you look at it, resemble skulls or masks. The sloping, undulating roof of the building, which has the appearance of being coated in scales, is supposed to be symbolic of a dragon, and the cross that sits atop the structure is suggestive of a knight's sword.

The rooms on the inside are every bit as stunning as the outside of the building. Gaudi was responsible for designing every aspect of the building, including the curved walls and ceilings, ornate woodwork, and stained glass windows. Visitors have the opportunity to take part in a guided tour of the house, during which they will gain insight into the history of the structure as well as Gaudi's design process.

The Noble Floor, which was intended to be used for hosting guests, is without a doubt one of the house's most magnificent rooms. The living space is characterized by a magnificent fireplace, intricate woodwork, and an elegant ceiling adorned with gold leaf. The light that comes into the space is diffused as it passes through the stained glass windows, resulting in an environment that is vibrant and almost enchanted.

Another highlight of the property is the rooftop terrace, which provides breathtaking vistas of the surrounding city. The area is embellished with chimneys that have the appearance of soldiers wearing helmets; this is another tribute to the whimsical aesthetic of Gaudi.

Taking in the sights and sounds of Casa Batllo is an unforgettable experience. This structure is a remarkable masterpiece of architecture and design, and it exemplifies Gaudi's brilliance as well as his ability to construct a space that is both beautiful and functional. It is an opportunity to experience the universe of one of the most recognized builders of all time, and as such, it is an attraction that should never be missed by anyone traveling to Barcelona.

The La Boqueria Market

In addition to its other name, Mercat de Sant Josep de la Boqueria, the La Boqueria Market is a lively marketplace that can be found in the center of Barcelona. It is one of those oldest and most popular marketplaces in the city, and it draws customers from within the city as well as from beyond the city. The market has a long and illustrious history, reaching all the way back to the 13th century when it first began as a mobile marketplace where items such as animals and vegetables were traded.

Today, La Boqueria Market is a permanent fixture in Barcelona. It is known for selling a diverse selection of fresh fruit, meats, seafood, and other specialties from the region. The hours of operation for the market are as follows: 8:00 am to 8:30 pm, Monday through Saturday; closed on Sundays and government holidays.

As you make your way around the market, you will be astounded by the wide selection of foods that are available for purchase. Your senses will be titillated by the brilliant colors and the fresh fragrances, and you will find it difficult to resist the desire to sample everything that is on offer.

The freshness of the market's produce, particularly its seafood, has earned it a reputation for being of the highest possible quality. You may buy anything from oysters and mussels to squid and octopus at the several stands that are located here. La Boqueria is an establishment that you simply must go to if you have a passion for fish.

Additionally, there is a vast assortment of cheeses and cured meats available at the market. You get the opportunity to sample the renowned Iberian ham from Spain, which is frequently regarded as the best ham in the world. Chorizo, fuet, and llonganissa are a few of the other delectable dishes that are considered to be regional delicacies.

In the event that you are experiencing feelings of hunger, there are numerous vendors that serve cooked foods such as Spanish omelets, paella, and tapas. You can surely grab a bite to eat while observing the bustling vitality of the market. There are many options.

The variety of goods that are sold at La Boqueria Market is undeniably one of the most striking aspects of this market. In addition to the regional specialties, you may get your hands on some of the most unusual fruits and vegetables from all over the world. The market is an accurate representation of the dynamic culture as well as the culinary traditions of Barcelona.

La Boqueria Market is a must-visit place in Barcelona. It is a place where you may delight in the freshest fruit and learn about the city's long and illustrious history in the culinary arts. It is imperative that you come along with both a healthy appetite and a spirit of exploration.

Discovery The Magic Fountain of Montjuic

The Magic Fountain of Montjuic is an amazing attraction that tourists to Barcelona should not pass up the chance to see. The fountain can be found in the district of Montjuic, and it features an incredible display of water, lights, and music that is guaranteed to amaze everyone who gets the chance to see it.

The fountain was initially constructed in 1929 for the International Exhibition, and ever since then, it has been one of the most visited attractions in the area. The fountain underwent a makeover in the 1980s, and since then, it has been one of the most well-known sights in the city.

Every evening, there is a performance put on by the fountain, which consists of a coordinated display of water, lights, and music. The program can be viewed for no charge and typically lasts for about twenty minutes. Throughout the course of the presentation, the illumination of the fountain takes on a myriad of colors and patterns, each of which is unique. The music is also chosen with great care so that it complements the atmosphere and pace of the water display.

Both the viewing space in front of the fountain and the steps that are located nearby provide guests with excellent vantage points from which to see the performance. Because of the potential for crowding in the viewing area, it is in your best interest to arrive as early as possible. The fountain is accessible to people using wheelchairs, and there are numerous seats and other lounging spots in the surrounding area.

The fountain can be found in the area of Montjuic, which is also the location of a number of other tourist destinations, such as the Montjuic Castle, the National Art Museum of Catalonia, and the Olympic Stadium. Exploring the neighborhood and taking in the sights is the kind of activity that can easily fill up a whole day for tourists.

The Magic Fountain of Montjuic is a must-see attraction in Barcelona, and visiting it at the end of the day, after having spent the day experiencing the city's many other sights and attractions, is a wonderful way to cap off the day. Consequently, when you go to Barcelona, you shouldn't forget to put it on your schedule so that you can witness the magic for yourself.

Visiting The Tibidabo

A mountain known as Tibidabo may be found on the outskirts of Barcelona. From its vantage point, one can see both the city and the Mediterranean Sea. At the peak of the mountain, guests will find a chapel, an amusement park, and a panoramic view of the city that is nothing short of breathtaking.

Since it first opened its gates in 1901, Tibidabo Amusement Park has the distinction of being one of the world's oldest continuously operating amusement parks. It provides access to a number of different rides, such as a Ferris wheel, a roller coaster, and a haunted house. In addition, guests have the opportunity to experience the park's more traditional rides and attractions, such as the airplane ride, the carousel, and the funhouse.

The mountain is not only home to the amusement park but also to the breathtaking Temple Expiatori del Sagrat Cor, which is a church that can be viewed from many different locations in the city. The construction of the church took place between the years 1902 and 1961, and it was designed in a neogothic style with Art Nouveau details. The view of the city from the top of the church's tower is even more impressive for guests who make the ascent.

Tramvia Blau is a vintage tram that connects the base of the mountain to the funicular station and allows guests to travel to Tibidabo using this mode of transportation. From that point, guests can ride a cable car all the way to the peak of the mountain. The trip there is an attraction in and of itself, as tourists get to take in the breathtaking scenery of the city and the countryside that surrounds it.

Tibidabo is a wonderful destination to spend a day with family and friends, enjoying the rides, the views, and the stunning architecture that is present throughout the park. It is also a favorite place for residents to gather to take in the beauty of their city while watching the sun go down. Tibidabo is a wonderful place to visit whether you're interested in history, the natural world, or both. There's something for everyone here.

Enjoying the Beaches of Barcelona

Not only is Barcelona a city rich in culture and architecture, but it is also a city with some of the most gorgeous beaches in the world. It is the ideal location, with its mild year-round temperature and abundant sunshine, for lounging on the beach and soaking up the sun of the Mediterranean. The following are a few of Barcelona's most popular and beautiful beaches:

Barceloneta Beach
A Guide to Enjoying Barcelona's Iconic Beach

Barceloneta is regarded as one of the city's most emblematic beaches and is among the city's many gorgeous beaches. This beach, which can be found in the district of Barceloneta, is not only simple to get to but also provides a wealth of recreational and calming options for visitors.

How to Get There

Barceloneta Beach can be reached quickly and easily by using either the metro or the bus from the heart of the city. The beach is only a few short blocks away from the Barceloneta metro stop, which is also conveniently located near various bus lines that stop close. If you would rather walk, From the city center, it should take you between 20 and 30 minutes to get there.

How to Proceed

Barceloneta Beach is full of fun things to do, so you won't be bored there. At any one time, there are quite a few people present at the beach. The following is a list of activities that are available to you at this beach:

Enjoy the warmth of the sun: Barceloneta Beach, with its expansive stretch of golden sand, is the ideal location for basking in the warmth of the sun that rises over the

Mediterranean. You can choose to relax by either laying out a towel on the sand or renting chairs and umbrellas from one of the many vendors that are located on the beach.

Take a dip in the water: The water in the sea off of Barceloneta Beach is often calm and warm, making it an excellent location for going for a swim. Because there are lifeguards on duty, you do not need to worry about your safety while you are having fun in the water.

Play a game of beach volleyball: Barceloneta Beach features multiple beach volleyball courts, so if you're in the mood for some exercise, you can grab a ball and get the game started.

Participate in one of the several water sports that are offered at Barceloneta Beach. These include windsurfing, paddleboarding, and jet skiing. The many merchants that are located on the beach offer both the ability to rent equipment and to take instruction.

Barceloneta Beach is lined with pubs and restaurants that serve up wonderful food and drinks that are refreshing. Enjoy the food and drink that is offered. You will have a wide variety of choices available to you, whether you are looking for something to eat in a hurry or something more substantial to satisfy your appetite.

Definitely not to be missed, the sunsets at Barceloneta Beach are among the most beautiful in the world. Take a seat at one of the beach bars, get a drink, and enjoy the show as the sun goes down below the horizon.

A Few Pointers for Your Trip

As earlier said, One of the most famous beaches in Barcelona is Barceloneta Beach, which means that it may get rather busy, especially during the high season. Be sure to come prepared for the throngs.

A word of warning: pickpockets can be a problem in any crowded tourist area, so make sure you look out for them. Always keep your things close to you, and always be mindful of your environment.

Sunscreen should be used: The sun in Barcelona may be very intense; therefore, it is important to protect your skin by using a sufficient amount of sunscreen.

Please help maintain the cleanliness of the beach by putting your rubbish in the receptacles that have been provided for that purpose.

In general, a trip to Barceloneta Beach should be included in the itinerary of everybody who is going to Barcelona. It is the ideal site to spend a day soaking up the sun and experiencing everything that Barcelona has to offer because of its gorgeous beach, warm sea, and bustling environment.

Nova Icaria Beach

The Nova Icaria Beach in Barcelona is a well-kept secret that can be found very near the Olympic Village. This is the perfect place for people who want to mix a day at the beach with a trip to nearby attractions.

Those looking to get away from the madding crowds will find that this beach is a better option than other of the more popular beaches in the city because it has a lower number of visitors. It is also a more peaceful beach, making it an excellent choice for families with children as well as individuals who like a more tranquil experience while at the beach.

Showers, changing rooms, and beach umbrellas and chairs that can be hired are some of the amenities that can be found at Nova Icaria Beach, which is well-equipped with such facilities. In addition, there are a great number of restaurants and cafes in the area, all of which offer mouthwatering cuisine and energizing beverages.

The beach is a great place to participate in a variety of water sports, such as paddleboarding, kayaking, and windsurfing. Visitors have the opportunity to rent gear and receive instruction from trained professionals.

The beach volleyball courts at Nova Icaria Beach are one of the attractions that visitors should not miss. The beach frequently plays host to competitions and other events, making it a fantastic location for socializing with new people and having a good time.

People who want to enjoy a day at the beach but don't want to deal with crowds will find that Nova Icaria Beach is an excellent option. It is very necessary to pay it a visit in order to take advantage of the breathtaking scenery, placid seas, and other facilities available there.

Bogatell Beach
A Peaceful Retreat in the Heart of Barcelona

When you think of Barcelona, the first thing that might come to mind is the city's exciting nightlife, the city's breathtaking architecture, or the city's rich history. Did you know that Barcelona, which is located in Spain, is home to some of the most beautiful beaches in all of Europe? Bogatell Beach is one of these undiscovered treasures; it is a peaceful haven that provides a much-needed escape from the frenetic activity of the city.

Bogatell Beach is a long and wide expanse of sand that is ideal for sunbathing, swimming, and resting, and it is found in the hip area of Poblenou. Bogatell is a beach that, in contrast to the more congested and touristy beaches such as Barceloneta, is a favorite destination for residents who like the laid-back ambiance and beautiful waters of the beach.

The fact that Bogatell Beach can be reached with relative ease by using public transportation is among its many attractive features. You may reach the beach by taking the metro to the Poblenou station and then walking for around ten minutes from there. You also have the option of taking the bus or renting a bike and going for a lovely ride along the promenade that runs along the water's edge.

When you get there, you'll be met by a beach that's not only wide but also very expansive and offers plenty of room for lounging in the sun. Because there is such a large selection of services to choose from, such as showers, baths, and sun loungers, it is very convenient to spend the entire day in this location. You may also take sailing lessons, rent paddleboards, and kayaks, or paddle around in one of these watercraft to get a better look at the pristine waterways.

There are lots of pubs and restaurants that line the promenade for those who want to take a break from the sun. These establishments serve a variety of cuisine and drinks, ranging from fresh seafood to ice-cold cocktails. In addition, if you are in need of some retail therapy, you can go shopping at the neighboring El Centre de la Vila shopping complex, which features a wide selection of brands from both the local and worldwide markets.

Bogatell Beach is a hidden treasure that is well worth a visit if you are searching for a calm refuge in the middle of Barcelona. The beach is located in the Bogatell neighborhood of Barcelona. This gorgeous beach is likely to take your breath away with its breathtaking landscape, regardless of whether you are a guest from out of town or a lifelong resident of the area, serene vibe, and convenient location. Be sure to bring some sun protection with you, and get ready to bask in the rays of the sun on one of the best-kept secrets in Barcelona.

Sant Sebastia Beach

There is a solid reason why the beach of Sant Sebastia is considered to be one of the most iconic beaches in Barcelona. Because of its enviable location in the center of the city, it is not only simple to reach but also provides a comprehensive selection of amenities that guests may take advantage of during their stay.

Sant Sebastia Beach is Barcelona's oldest and largest beach, and it has a long history of being a popular destination for tourists as well as locals. It is convenient to get to on foot, by bicycle, or by using the public transportation system because it is located just a few minutes away from the Barceloneta district.

The beach itself is expansive and roomy, providing plenty of room for sunbathing, playing beach activities, or just unwinding with a nice book and a decent cup of coffee. Because the water is completely clear and excellent for swimming, this is an excellent location for families that have young children. After a day spent lounging in the warm rays of the sun, guests will appreciate the beach's availability of showers, restrooms, and changing rooms where they may clean up.

The proximity to a diverse selection of dining options, including cafés, pubs, and restaurants, is undoubtedly one of the highlights of Sant Sebastia Beach. While taking in the breathtaking scenery of the Mediterranean, guests can relax with a tasty meal or a refreshing drink at this restaurant.

Paddleboarding, kayaking, and windsurfing are just a few of the many water activities that may be enjoyed by visitors to the beach who are looking to spice up their vacation with a little bit of excitement. Visitors have the option of renting equipment from local businesses or going on a tour with a guide in order to investigate the shoreline.

Anyone who wants to get the most out of their time spent at Barcelona's beaches should make it a point to spend some time at Sant Sebastia Beach. It is the ideal place to relax in the warm rays of the sun and take in the splendor of the Mediterranean, thanks to its great location, breathtaking views, and extensive choice of amenities.

Barcelona Travel Guide 2023 & Beyond

Chapter 4: Barcelona's Food and Drink Scene

The cuisine and drink scene in Barcelona is a vibrant and eclectic blend of traditional Catalan cuisine, inventive fusion dishes, and cuisines from around the world. The city is well-known for its gastronomic options, including a huge selection of restaurants, cafes, and bars that cater to a variety of preferences and price points. There is something for everyone in Barcelona, from restaurants with Michelin stars to vendors selling food on the street.

Paella, a rice dish traditionally prepared in Barcelona with saffron and a wide variety of meats, seafood, and vegetables, is considered to be one of the city's signature foods and should not be missed. It is a fundamental component of Spanish cuisine and may be discovered in a wide variety of restaurants all across the city. Tapas, which are little plates of food, is another classic dish. These plates of food are ideal for sharing with friends while drinking a glass of wine or beer.

The city of Barcelona is home to a wide variety of fusion cuisines, which combine the flavors and ingredients that are traditionally associated with Catalan cuisine with those of other cultures. Tickets Bar, owned and operated by the Adria brothers, is one of the most well-known restaurants in the city due to the avant-garde and creative cuisine it serves. Classic Spanish cuisine, such as liquid olives, Iberian ham croquettes, and foie gras lollipops, are reimagined in a way that is both whimsical and inventive by this restaurant.

In addition to its cuisine, Barcelona is well-known for the drinking culture that it has developed. Rioja, Ribera del Duero, and Priorat are just a few of the regions in Spain that are renowned for their wine production and are responsible for creating some of the best wines in the country. There is also a thriving cocktail scene in Barcelona, with numerous establishments serving original and forward-thinking drinks that are prepared using regional ingredients.

Beer fans will be pleased to know that Barcelona has a burgeoning craft beer culture, with an increasing number of local brewers and taprooms opening their doors all across the city. Beer lovers frequently congregate at Moritz since it is a local brewery that was established in 1856. In addition to providing tours of both their brewery and taproom, they sell a range of craft beers and a selection of food.

A journey to Barcelona would not be complete without at least one stop at a traditional bodega, which is a pub that serves tapas and wine from the region. These quaint and quiet taverns offer a glimpse of Barcelona's bygone era, complete with a selection of regional wines, vermouth, and traditional Catalan foods.

The cuisine and beverage scene in Barcelona is an accurate reflection of the city's culture and history. The city is home to a wide variety of restaurants, serving up anything from classic Catalan fare to cutting-edge fusion creations. Barcelona is a great gastronomic destination that one should not skip out on visiting because of the city's impressively vibrant and diversified culinary offers.

The best places to eat in Barcelona

The following are some of Barcelona's most well-regarded dining establishments, along with their addresses, services, telephone numbers, and website links:

Tickets:

Address: Avinguda del Paral·lel, 164, 08015 Barcelona

Services: Spanish cuisine, tapas, cocktails

Phone: +34 932 92 42 53

Website: https://www.ticketsbar.es/en/home/

Bar Canete:

Address: Carrer de la Unió, 17, 08001 Barcelona

Services: Catalan cuisine, tapas, wine

Phone: +34 933 17 30 94

Website: https://www.barcanete.com/en/home/

Disfrutar:

Address: Carrer de Villarroel, 163, 08036 Barcelona

Services: Mediterranean cuisine, creative dishes

Phone: +34 933 48 68 96

Website: https://www.disfrutarbarcelona.com/en/

El Quim de la Boqueria:

Address: Mercado de la Boqueria, La Rambla, 91, 08001 Barcelona

Services: Catalan cuisine, seafood, tapas

Phone: +34 933 17 31 20

Website: https://www.elquimdelaboqueria.com/

Dos Palillos:

Address: Carrer d'Elisabets, 9, 08001 Barcelona

Services: Asian cuisine, tapas, sake

Phone: +34 935 10 94 34

Website: https://www.dospalillos.com/

Cervecería Catalana:

Address: Carrer de Mallorca, 236, 08008 Barcelona

Services: Spanish cuisine, tapas, beer

Phone: +34 932 16 03 68

Website: https://www.cerveceriacatalana.com/en/

Bar Mut:

Address: Carrer de Pau Claris, 192, 08037 Barcelona

Services: Spanish cuisine, tapas, cocktails

Phone: +34 932 17 43 11

Website: https://www.barmut.com/

Pakta:

Address: Carrer de Lleida, 5, 08004 Barcelona

Services: Peruvian-Japanese fusion, tasting menu

Phone: +34 936 24 92 70

Website: https://www.pakta.es/

Can Solé:

Address: Carrer de Sant Carles, 4, 08003 Barcelona

Services: Catalan cuisine, seafood, paella

Phone: +34 932 21 50 12

Website: https://cansole.cat/

Casa Calvet:

Address: Carrer de Casp, 48, 08010 Barcelona

Services: Catalan cuisine, fine dining

Phone: +34 933 17 30 32

Website: https://www.casacalvet.es/en/

These eateries provide diners with a selection of cuisines to choose from as well as a variety of dining experiences, ranging from laid-back tapas bars to upscale dining locations. These restaurants provide some of the finest examples of Catalan and Spanish cuisine and should not be missed by visitors to Barcelona. Some of the local delicacies that should not be missed are paella, ham from the Iberian peninsula, and fresh seafood.

Barcelona Travel Guide 2023 & Beyond

Chapter 5: Shopping in Barcelona

The city of Barcelona is a shopper's dream, with a wide range of choices to suit a variety of preferences and price points. There is a shopping experience to suit everyone's preferences, from upscale designer stores to classic marketplaces and quaint independent businesses. The following are some of the top shopping destinations in Barcelona:

- *Passeig de Gracia:* Passeig de Gracia is widely considered to be one of the most opulent and high-class shopping alleys in all of Barcelona. It is home to renowned luxury labels such as Chanel, Gucci, and

Louis Vuitton, in addition to local designers and high-end businesses of their own creation.

- *La Roca Village:* La Roca Village is an open-air shopping mall with over 130 boutiques selling designer apparel, accessories, and homeware. It is located just outside of Barcelona. La Roca Village is known as a popular tourist destination. It is an excellent location to go to in order to find sales on high-end brands like Armani, Prada, and Versace.

- *El Corte Ingles:* El Corte Ingles is the most well-known department store chain in Spain; it can be discovered in a number of different sites across the city of Barcelona. It is a one-stop shop for all kinds of goods, ranging from apparel and accessories to consumer electronics, kitchenware, and even food. In addition, the flagship store on Placa de Catalunya has a gourmet food market located on the ground floor of the building.

- *Mercat de la Boqueria*: Mercat de la Boqueria: This well-known market is not only a wonderful place to purchase fresh fruit, meats, and seafood, but it is also a wonderful spot to sample regional specialties such as Iberian ham and Spanish omelets. In addition, there are a great number of stalls offering various goods, including mementos.

- *Portal de l'Angel:* This pedestrian thoroughfare in the center of the city is lined with shops selling apparel, shoes, and accessories from well-known brands like Zara, H&M, and Mango, amongst others. It is a fantastic location for shopping that is kind to one's wallet.

- *Encants Vells:* With a history that dates all the way back to the 14th century, this is one of the oldest flea markets in all of Europe. It is a wonderful location to go to if you are looking for antiques, vintage apparel, or any other one-of-a-kind products.

- *Gracia Neighborhood:* The Gracia district is a bohemian district that is home to a large number of local designers and independent boutiques. These shops sell a wide variety of items, ranging from one-of-a-kind apparel and accessories to handcrafted jewelry.

- *Rambla de Catalunya:* This boulevard is home to a wide variety of local and worldwide brands, in addition to a number of more specialized, locally-owned shops. The atmosphere is perfect for taking a leisurely stroll and doing some window shopping.

It doesn't matter if you're looking for high-end designer goods, one-of-a-kind local boutiques, or old-school marketplaces; Barcelona has plenty to offer shoppers who prefer any and all of these types of shopping experiences. Let's put that behind us and examine the various shopping districts now.

Passeig de Gracia

One of the most famous avenues in Barcelona, Passeig de Gracia is renowned for its elegant stores and stunning buildings, making it one of the city's most recognizable thoroughfares. Because it is situated in the middle of the city, it is an essential destination for everyone who has an interest in architecture or fashion.

A number of well-known architects, including Antoni Gaudi, Lluis Domenech I Montaner, and Josep Puig I Cadafalch, are responsible for the creation of the stunning structures that line this street. Casa Batllo, which was designed by Gaudi and featured an ornate and colorful facade, is without a doubt one of the buildings that is recognized all over the world. Another noteworthy structure is the Casa Amatller, which was created by Cadafalch and featured an impressive Art Nouveau style.

Passeig de Gracia is renowned not only for its stunning architecture but also for being home to a number of the most prestigious fashion houses in the world. In addition to local designers and upscale department shops like El Corte Ingles, tourists can shop at high-end boutiques like Chanel, Gucci, and Louis Vuitton. In addition, there are also local designers.

However, Passeig de Gracia isn't limited to just the high-end shoppers in Barcelona. There is a large selection of more reasonably priced options available, such as Zara and Mango, in addition to a variety of souvenir shops and artisanal stores providing hand-crafted items.

Additionally, the street is home to a diverse selection of eateries and cafes, which range from hip and contemporary to classic and homey in the atmosphere. While taking in the stunning architecture and people-watching, guests can savor a meal or a cup of coffee at the establishment.

The Passeig de Gracia is a wonderful area to spend the afternoon or evening, and it can be reached quickly and simply by both the metro and the bus. Passeig de Gracia is a destination that should not be skipped, regardless of whether you have a passion for fashion or architecture or whether you're just searching for a beautiful area to wander around.

La Roca Village

La Roca Village is the place to go shopping if you want to find high-end goods at outlet costs. If this is what you're looking for, then you've come to the right location. This open-air shopping mall is conveniently located just a short drive from Barcelona, and it features a diverse selection of high-end retailers offering discounts of up to 70% off the original price.

Over 130 different boutiques selling anything from designer clothing and accessories to homeware and beauty products can be found in the La Roca Village shopping center. Armani, Prada, Versace, and Burberry are just a few of the illustrious brands associated with the fashion industry that are featured here. Additionally, local Spanish designers such as Desigual and Adolfo Dominguez are featured.

One of the best aspects of La Roca Village is that it is an open-air mall; as a result, you can take advantage of the beautiful weather in Spain while you are doing your shopping there. The layout of the shopping center is really attractive, with broad pedestrianized pathways that are lined with palm palms and bright flowers. There is plenty of opportunities to take a break and unwind, including seating areas and fountains located outdoors.

La Roca Village has a variety of additional services and amenities, in addition to retail options, to ensure that your time there is as pleasurable and relaxing as it can be. In addition to a children's playground and a prayer room for those who feel the need for it, there are a number of restaurants and cafes in the area that serve both Spanish and other types of food from around the world.

It won't be difficult for you to make your way to La Roca Village if you're staying in Barcelona. A shuttle service, which runs daily and takes around forty minutes to reach the mall from the city center, is provided by the shopping complex. You may also choose to drive yourself to the location, as there is plenty of free parking accessible on the premises. Another option is to take a taxi.

It is highly recommended that you pay a visit to La Roca Village if you have a passion for fashion and are looking for discounts on high-end items. It is the ideal place to spend the day shopping in the sun due to its picturesque environment, an extensive selection of boutiques, and fantastic pricing.

El Corte Ingles

El Corte Ingles is a famous department store chain in Spain that has multiple locations in Barcelona. It is highly recommended that you go there. The retail network provides customers of all types, including visitors, with access to a comprehensive selection of goods and services designed to meet their individual requirements.

Placa de Catalunya is home to the El Corte Ingles main shop, which can be found smack dab in the middle of the action in the city. It is a structure with seven floors that sells a wide variety of goods, including food, apparel and accessories, consumer electronics, and home goods. The gourmet food market that is housed in the basement of this store is one of the primary draws that customers come to see. The market is a gastronome's dream come true because it carries such a diverse selection of fresh and unusual produce, regional and foreign specialties, as well as wines and spirits of the highest quality. It is a wonderful spot to pick up some regional wares to take back with you as mementos of your trip.

El Corte Ingles has numerous other sites throughout the city in addition to its main store, one of which can be found at the Diagonal Mar shopping mall, while another can be found in the La Rambla neighborhood. If you are searching for particular items, it is in your best interest to visit various stores because each one carries a selection of goods that is distinct from the others.

One of the many wonderful things about El Corte Ingles is that it allows customers who are not residents of the European Union to make purchases tax-free. This indicates that you will be able to claim a refund of the VAT (Value Added Tax) that was paid on any purchases made at the airport prior to departing the country. The procedure is easy to follow, and there are information desks located within the stores to provide assistance with the paperwork that must be completed.

"The Gallery" is the name of the specialized luxury department that can be found at El Corte Ingles; if you are a fan of high-end fashion labels, you will like shopping there. This section showcases unique collections from some of the world's most renowned fashion designers, including Dior, Gucci, and Armani, among others. Personal shoppers and stylists are available to assist you with your shopping requirements at The Gallery, which provides a tailored shopping experience for its customers.

When in Barcelona, a trip to the El Corte Ingles department store is one of the city's must-do activities for shoppers. This department store chain contains everything you could possibly need or want, including apparel, consumer electronics, home furnishings, food, and luxury goods. It is a quick and delightful shopping experience for tourists because there are several stores spread throughout the city, and tax-free shopping is available for anyone who does not live in the European Union.

Mercat de la Boqueria

Mercat de la Boqueria, often referred to as Mercat de Sant Josep de la Boqueria, is one of the most well-known markets in Barcelona. It is an absolute must-see for any foodie or traveler who wants to become fully immersed in the culture of the area they are visiting. This lively market has been operating continuously since the 13th century, making it one of the oldest in all of Europe. It can be found right in the middle of the Gothic Quarter of the city.

The market is home to more than 300 vendors that sell a diverse array of fresh and unusual produce, such as fruits, vegetables, meats, fish, cheeses, spices, and many more items. The sights, smells, and sounds of the market combine to create an exhilarating and stimulating environment for the senses.

The market is well-known not only for its fresh produce but also for its pubs and restaurants. These establishments provide tourists the opportunity to try regional specialties such as fresh fish, Iberian ham, and Spanish omelets. Because of its location in the heart of the city, the market is an ideal place to stop for a speedy breakfast or lunch while traveling around the city.

In addition to selling food, the Mercat de la Boqueria also sells a variety of other merchandise, including clothing, accessories, and souvenirs, among other things. Visitors will have the opportunity to purchase a wide variety of goods, ranging from handcrafted crafts and traditional ceramics to contemporary apparel and jewelry.

If you want to escape the crowds at the market, the ideal time to go is either very early in the morning or very late in the evening. This is especially true during the busiest time of the year for tourists. It is essential that you keep a close eye on your valuables at all times because there is a risk of pickpocketing in the neighborhood.

Anyone interested in enjoying the lively culture and food of Barcelona should make it a point to stop by Mercat de la Boqueria at some point during their trip. It is an excellent location to indulge in regional delicacies, search for one-of-a-kind mementos, and completely submerge oneself in the vibrant energy of the city.

Portal de l'Angel

Located in the middle of the Gothic Quarter in Barcelona is the street known as Portal de l'Angel, which is known as one of the busiest and most popular shopping avenues in the city. The street that is only accessible to pedestrians is bordered on both sides with a wide variety of shops, ranging from major international names to specialized local boutiques.

The street is home to a number of well-known Spanish high street retailers, such as Zara, H&M, and Mango, making it an ideal location for shoppers looking for reasonably priced clothing. You may get anything here, from clothes, shoes, and accessories to cosmetics and things to decorate your home with. The costs are affordable, and there are regular opportunities to save via sales and other promotions.

On Portal de l'Angel, you won't just find fashion boutiques; there are also a great many other kinds of shops to peruse. You can find anything from booksellers and gift shops to establishments specializing in technological goods and music here.

While you're out doing your shopping, you may take advantage of the many restaurants, cafes, and street entertainers that are located in the area. When there are a lot of people around, going shopping may be a very exciting and entertaining experience.

This is especially true at times of year when there are a lot of tourists.

Be prepared for large crowds and significant wait times because it is possible for this area to become packed, as is the case with any major shopping district. If you want to come without dealing with crowds, the best time to go is during the week during regular business hours.

If you are searching for a shopping experience that is both entertaining and within your price range in the middle of Barcelona, then you absolutely have to go to Portal de l'Angel.

Encants Vells

For those who are interested in vintage and antique shopping, Encants Vells, which is also known as Mercat Fira de Bellcaire, is an absolute necessity to visit. El Clot is a historic area in Barcelona, and its market is known for its long and illustrious history, which dates back to the 14th century.

Because of its enormous size, which is over 15,000 square meters, this market is considered to be one of the greatest flea markets in all of Europe. Encants Vells is a veritable treasure trove for anybody hunting for one-of-a-kind bargains since it features over 500 vendors selling a wide variety of items, including pre-owned apparel and accessories, antique books, vintage furniture, and more.

On Mondays, Wednesdays, Fridays, and Saturdays, the market is open; however, to avoid crowds, it is recommended that customers arrive as early as possible. It is recommended that if you are seeking a particular item, you take the time to go among the many stalls and booths. It is not unusual to stumble upon unique and one-of-a-kind items in this location.

The auction system that Encants Vells use is undoubtedly one of the game's defining characteristics. On Tuesdays and Thursdays of each week, there is a public auction that features valuable antiques and artifacts. The public is welcome to attend the auction, and those who do so will have the opportunity to experience the frenzy and activity that ensues as bids compete for highly desirable things.

In addition to being a fantastic site to go shopping, Encants Vells is also an excellent location for becoming fully immersed in the culture of the area. Because the market draws in a varied audience consisting of both locals and visitors, it is an excellent location at which to engage in people-watching and get a feel for the pulsating spirit of the city. You can also take a break and enjoy some refreshments at one of the many cafes or bars that are located in the area surrounding the market.

The Encants Vells market is a one-of-a-kind and fascinating place that provides a glimpse into the extensive history and culture of Barcelona. Whether you're a collector or just searching for a one-of-a-kind memento to remember your trip by, this location is fantastic for finding one-of-a-kind products. Every traveler who comes to Barcelona should make it a point to stop at Encants Vells due to the exciting ambiance and remarkable assortment of stalls that it offers.

Gracia Neighborhood

Gracia is a neighborhood in Barcelona that is located a short distance from the heart of the city and is known for its vibrancy and eclecticism. Because of its reputation for having a bohemian atmosphere, lovely squares, and tiny alleyways, it is a favorite destination not just among tourists but also among locals.

Gracia's shopping sector, which is home to a large number of local designers as well as numerous independent businesses, is one of the neighborhood's primary draws. Visitors have the chance to find out a diverse selection of one-of-a-kind articles of clothes, jewelry, and accessories that are not sold in larger chain stores. A couple of the most well-known shops in the area are Abansparis, which sells vintage apparel and accessories, and Rita Row, which focuses on providing modern clothing for women. Both of these shops are located on Rita Row.

Gracia is well-known not only for its retail establishments but also for its artistic vibe and active nightlife. Visitors will be able to enjoy live music, plays at the theater, and art exhibitions at the several galleries, theaters, and cultural centers that call this neighborhood home. The Placa del Sol is a lively square that is lined with outdoor cafes, bars, and restaurants; it is one of the most popular places to visit. While taking in the vibrant scene of the neighborhood, guests are welcome to have a meal or a drink at one of the local establishments.

Another location in Gracia that you just cannot miss is the Mercat de la Llibertat. This is a traditional market where guests can purchase a wide selection of handcrafted goods in addition to fresh fruit, meats, and seafood. It is a wonderful spot to become fully immersed in the culture of the area and to try some of the delectable cuisines that Catalonia has to offer.

Gracia is an extraordinary and enchanting area that provides a diverse selection of opportunities for shopping, dining, and experiencing the local culture. People who are searching for an alternative to the more touristy regions of Barcelona and a chance to experience the authentic side of the city will find that this is the ideal destination for them.

Rambla de Catalunya

One of the most well-known and well-liked areas for retail therapy in Barcelona is called Rambla de Catalunya. It runs parallel to the world-famous La Rambla and is situated in the very center of the Eixample neighborhood. Because the street is flanked on both sides by trees, benches, and restaurants, it is an ideal location for taking a leisurely stroll, people-watching, and shopping.

On Rambla de Catalunya, you'll find an incredible assortment of shops, ranging from family-owned boutiques to well-known multinational brands. Zara, Mango, and Massimo Dutti are three of the most well-known retailers in the world. These stores are known for selling fashionable clothing at reasonable prices for both men and women. You may discover fashionable footwear at a number of different shoe stores, such as Camper and Mascaró, among others.

In addition to retailers selling clothing, Rambla de Catalunya is home to a number of establishments selling home furnishings and accessories. While Vincon focuses on contemporary furniture and accessories, Natura Casa is known for selling a wide variety of one-of-a-kind and eco-friendly home items. Additionally, there are a variety of shops selling Catalan products like ceramics, leather goods, and gastronomy, which are perfect if you are searching for gifts or mementos to take home with you.

The Rambla de Catalunya is notable for the numerous cafes and eateries that can be found throughout its length. You may sit back and relax with a meal or a cup of coffee on one of the many outdoor terraces, while also enjoying the sights and sounds of the area. Cafe Zurich, which has been a gathering place for locals since the 1920s, and La Crema Canela, which serves wonderful pastries and desserts, are two of the most popular places to go. Cafe Zurich has been there for almost a century.

The Eixample neighborhood is home to some of the city's most stunning buildings, and Rambla de Catalunya is a wonderful area to stroll around and take it all in while also getting a taste of the local shopping culture. This street caters to everyone's needs, whether they be for apparel, wares for the home, or simply a stroll in a nice environment.

Chapter 6: Day Trips from Barcelona

There are numerous alternatives for day trips that can be embarked upon from Barcelona, It's a great place to start exploring the area, which makes it a great place to stay.

These are some of the most popular places that you should think about visiting:

Montserrat: Montserrat is a mountain range that is about an hour's drive from Barcelona and is home to a Benedictine monastery in addition to having a breathtaking natural landscape. To get to the summit of the mountain, where there are panoramic views, visitors can ride a cable car or a funicular.

Sitges: Sitges is a picturesque coastal town that is well-known for its stunning beaches, winding streets, and brightly colored buildings that it has. It is an excellent location to get away from the commotion of the city and enjoy some leisure by the water in this beautiful setting.

Girona: Girona, a city steeped in history, can be reached from Barcelona by car in about an hour and a half. It is famous for its Gothic architecture, its gorgeous Onyar River, and its Jewish quarter, which has been carefully conserved.

The Costa Brava: This is a breathtaking length of coastline that can be found roughly two hours outside of Barcelona. It is famous for the steep cliffs, secluded bays, and pure seas that can be found there. Visitors get the opportunity to taste the fresh seafood and explore the picturesque fishing communities.

Tarragona: This historic Roman city is roughly an hour's drive from Barcelona. It is known for its gastronomy. It is the location of ruins that have been carefully preserved, including an amphitheater, an aqueduct, and ancient fortifications.

No matter the day excursion you decide to take, the areas surrounding Barcelona offer a wealth of sights and activities to discover.

At this point, we are going to examine each of them in further depth.

A Day trip to Montserrat

Montserrat is an absolutely breathtaking mountain range that is situated about an hour's drive west of Barcelona, and a trip there is highly recommended. The name "Montserrat" literally means "serrated mountain," which is appropriate given the jagged peaks that make up the range.

The Benedictine monastery of Montserrat, which has been there since the 11th century, may be found at the very peak of the mountain. The monastery is still operational in the modern day, and there are approximately 80 monks who live and work there. People who come to the monastery may go on tours and view the stunning basilica, which is home to the renowned Black Madonna. This is a statue of the Virgin Mary carved out of wood that is said to have amazing healing properties.

Taking the cable car or the funicular up Montserrat is among the most efficient ways to reach the peak of the island. The views of the surrounding countryside that are available from either choice are stunning. When they reach the peak, tourists can take a hike through the mountains and take in the breathtaking views of the surrounding landscape. There are a number of different hiking trails to choose from, each with a different level of difficulty, so everyone can find something they like.

There are a number of other places of interest in Montserrat that are well worth visiting, in addition to the monastery and the island's breathtaking natural scenery. Both the Montserrat Museum and the Montserrat Audiovisual Space provide visitors with the opportunity to participate in a multimedia experience that narrates the history of the mountain and the monastery. The Montserrat Museum has a collection of art from ancient times up to the current day.

Anyone who is in Barcelona should absolutely make time to go on a day excursion to Montserrat. Montserrat has something for everyone to enjoy, whether it is the island's rich history, its abundant natural beauty, or just its breathtaking vistas.

A Day Trip to Sitges
Sitges: A Quaint Coastal Getaway from Barcelona

The picturesque coastal town of Sitges is only 35 kilometers to the southwest of Barcelona, making it a favorite destination for day trips from the city of Barcelona, as well as for tourists. Sitges is a wonderful spot to get away from the bustle and hustle of the city and enjoy some relaxation by the sea. It is famous for its picturesque beaches, winding alleyways, and brightly colored buildings.

The beaches of Sitges are often considered to be one of the city's most appealing features. Visitors have their pick of 17 distinct beaches, so the variety of options is sure to please. Platja de la Ribera and Platja de San Sebastian are two of the most popular beaches in the area. Platja de la Ribera can be found in the middle of the city and offers a wide variety of services. Platja de San Sebastian is located to the east of the city and is a quieter beach. Platja de la Barra, Platja de la Fragata, and Platja de Balmins are a few of the other beaches in the area that are well worth a visit.

In addition to its beaches, Sitges is well-known for its ancient town, which is comprised of winding alleyways, charming squares, and brightly colored buildings. The Church of Sant Bartomeu I Santa Tecla, which can be found on top of a hill with a view of the ocean, is regarded as one of the most important landmarks in the town. Visitors have the opportunity to ascend the bell tower and take in breathtaking vistas of the surrounding area, including the shoreline.

Sitges is particularly well-known for the vibrant cultural scene that it possesses. Throughout the course of the year, the town plays host to a number of festivals, the most notable of which are the International Fantastic Film Festival of Catalonia, the Sitges Carnival, and the Sitges Wine Festival. In addition, tourists can enjoy perusing the several art galleries and museums located inside the city, such as the Cau Ferrat Museum, which is home to the works of the sculptor Santiago Rusiol.

It is not difficult to get to Sitges from Barcelona. Sitges can be reached from the Sants Station in Barcelona in a little over half an hour by taking one of the frequent trains that run between the two cities. The Estació del Nord bus station in Barcelona also offers a bus service, and the travel time for this route is around forty-five minutes.

Sitges is an excellent location to visit if you want to get away from the commotion of Barcelona and enjoy some relaxation by the water. Anyone who is going to be in the area should make it a point to stop there at some point because it has some stunning beaches, a fascinating historic center, and a thriving cultural scene.

A Day trip to Girona

Girona: A Beautiful Day Trip from Barcelona

Girona is a picturesque city that is the ideal destination for a day trip, and it can be reached from Barcelona in over an hour and a half by rail. Those who are interested in discovering more of Catalonia beyond the city of Barcelona should make it a point to stop at Girona. This city is known for its extensive history as well as its stunning architecture. These are some of the most memorable aspects of a trip to Girona:

Old Town: The medieval and Gothic buildings in Girona's old town have been meticulously conserved, and the area is characterized by a labyrinth of winding streets and lanes. Visitors have the opportunity to stroll through the Jewish Quarter, take in the magnificent city walls and towers, and investigate the many museums and galleries located in the surrounding area.

Cathedral of Girona: The Cathedral of Girona is a magnificent example of Gothic architecture, and it can be discovered in the center of the old town of Girona. The cathedral was constructed in the 14th century and is known for its magnificent cloister as well as its magnificent nave.

Arab Baths: The Arab Baths are an excellent example of Moorish architecture in Spain, and they have been successfully kept over the years. During the time that the Arabs occupied Spain, these vaulted ceilings, columns, and pools served as places of leisure and purification. Visitors can view these features today.

Onyar River: The Onyar River flows through the middle of Girona, and its banks are adorned with vividly colored houses that provide a magnificent backdrop for a promenade along the river. The river itself is a popular tourist attraction in the city.

Food & Wine: Girona is well-known for its outstanding food and wine scene, and the surrounding area features a large number of restaurants and wineries that have earned Michelin stars. Guests have the opportunity to try regional delicacies such as botifarra sausage, truffles, and cava, a sparkling wine that is produced in Catalonia.

Girona has much to offer everyone, regardless of whether they are interested in history, architecture, gastronomy, wine, etc. Because of its close proximity to Barcelona as well as the stunning scenery that it offers, it is the ideal location for a day trip.

A Day trip to Costa Brava

The Costa Brava is an excellent place to go on a day trip if you want to get away from the hectic pace of Barcelona. This breathtaking length of coastline can be found approximately two hours north of the city. It is famous for the craggy cliffs, secret coves, and gin-clear waters that can be found there.

Renting a car and making your way around the Costa Brava's winding coastal roads is one of the most enjoyable ways to get to know this region of Spain. Along the route, you'll come across quaint fishing communities like Calella de Palafrugell and Tamariu, both of which provide delicious locally caught seafood and the chance to fully immerse oneself in the local culture.

Tossa de Mar is a village on the Costa Brava that is renowned for its ancient castle as well as its scenic beach, and it's considered to be one of the region's most iconic locations. TThe fortress was constructed in the twelfth century, has breathtaking vistas of the surrounding area, including the sea and the town. In addition to being a popular place for swimming and sunbathing, the beach is also home to a large number of restaurants and bars in the immediate area.

Those who are looking for a more physically demanding vacation will find a plethora of chances for kayaking and trekking all along the Costa Brava. The Camino de Ronda is a trail that travelers often choose to walk since it follows the coast and provides stunning vistas of the Mediterranean Sea. You may also go on guided kayaking tours, which give you the opportunity to explore the secluded coves and underwater caves that are dotted along the coast.

Those who are hoping to get away from the bustle and hustle of the city and take in the breathtaking scenery of the Catalan coastline can consider making a day trip to the Costa Brava. Along this breathtaking stretch of coast, there is something for everyone to enjoy, whether their passion lies in the exploration of the great outdoors, learning about local history, or participating in cultural activities.

A Day trip to Tarragona

Approximately one hour's drive from Barcelona will bring you to the medieval city of Tarragona. Tarragona was established by the Romans in the third century BC, and the city is currently home to a sizeable collection of Roman ruins. These ruins have been carefully kept and offer a look into the city's extensive past.

The Roman Amphitheater in Tarragona is one of the city's most popular tourist destinations. It was constructed in the second century AD and has a capacity of up to 15,000 audience members. Today, tourists are free to explore the ruins of the amphitheater and conjure up images of the gladiatorial contests and other events that used to take place there in days gone by.

The ancient walls of Tarragona are another renowned tourist destination. These walls were constructed in the second century BC and previously encircled the entire city. Walks along the city walls allow guests to take in breathtaking vistas of both the city and the Mediterranean Sea.

A well-preserved aqueduct was constructed in Tarragona in the first century AD with the purpose of supplying the city with water. This aqueduct may be found in the city. The remarkable feats of engineering and architecture that were accomplished in the construction of the aqueduct, which is more than 4 kilometers long, can be viewed by tourists.

In addition to its Roman ruins, the old town of Tarragona is a picturesque neighborhood that features winding lanes, historic houses, and an abundance of cafes and restaurants. Visitors can take in the history and culture of this old city while strolling around the streets of the town.

History enthusiasts and anybody interested in ancient Roman civilization will enjoy a day trip or weekend break to Tarragona, which is easily accessible from Barcelona by rail or bus. Tarragona is an excellent destination for anyone interested in the ancient Roman civilization.

Barcelona Travel Guide 2023 & Beyond

Chapter 7: How to stay safe in Barcelona

How safe is it to go to Barcelona? Is it safe for people to go to Barcelona in terms of general crime?

By foreign standards, Barcelona is still thought to be a safe place to visit.

Most people also think that public transportation, the Metro, and taxis are safe from violent crime and reliable for residents and guests to use.

When you walk around, you get the sense that Barcelona is still a safe and friendly place where both locals and visitors look and feel happy and at ease.

Most parts of the city don't feel dangerous during the day.

Still, there is some crime, and there are terror risks, just like in any modern city.

Mostly, it is safe to get cash from an ATM, but you should always be aware of your surroundings and be careful to hide your PIN number.

Be careful if you get cash late at night or early in the morning by yourself, and try not to do it.

If you wear an expensive watch on your wrist, you should be careful.

When you check in or out of a hotel, keep your bags in front of you.

People should be careful to avoid small thefts because pickpockets are a known problem in Barcelona. Few years before now, there has been a rise in violent small crimes.

For 2023, if you need to be extra careful late at night, you should avoid the Raval area of the old city.

In general, violent crime levels are low compared to other big cities, and the police are working to stop the rise in violent crime, but you should still be careful.

We advise tourists to be careful when wearing expensive watches near high-end hotels, shopping areas, and popular nightclubs in upscale neighborhoods. Few years before now, it has been seen that more and more criminal gangs are going after expensive personal items.

When you drive by car, don't leave valuable things out in the open, even in underground parking lots.

In general, the only part of Barcelona where you should be extra careful late at night is in the lower part of the Raval area of the city's old medieval city and maybe also at the port end of La Rambla. However, even in these areas, violent crimes are rare during the day and evening. Most crimes are small, like stealing a bag, but serious crimes are rare.

Security alerts

In August 2019, the U.S. Consulate General in Barcelona sent out a Security Alert telling U.S. citizens:

"An increase in violent crime in the city of Barcelona in the summer of 2019, especially in tourist areas. Local authorities have reported a significant increase in the number of petty theft schemes that include acts of violence, such as aggressive thefts of jewelry, watches, and purses. In some cases, these incidents have led to injuries. Authorities say they are working to fix these problems."

"Nearly 19 million British people went to Spain last year, and most of them had a good time," says the U.K. Foreign Office website.

The Economist Intelligence Unit's (EIU) "Safe Cities Index 2017" showed that Barcelona was one of the safest places in the world when it came to general crime and was ranked 13th in the world overall.

Barcelona was named the fourth safest city in the European Union and the fifth safest city in all of Europe. This meant that in 2017, Barcelona was only less safe than Stockholm, Amsterdam, Zurich, and Madrid in terms of general safety.

In the 2018 TripAdvisor Travelers' Choice Destinations Awards, Barcelona came in sixth place as one of the top ten towns in the world that TripAdvisor users liked best. Several places in Spain are on this TripAdvisor list, which shows that Spain is a top place to visit and is safe to do so.

The Economist Intelligence Unit's (EIU) "Safe Cities Index 2019" showed that Barcelona was one of the safest cities in the world in terms of general crime. It placed 19th in the world for personal safety and 26th overall.

In the 2018 TripAdvisor Travelers' Choice Destinations Awards, Barcelona came in sixth place as one of the top ten towns in the world that TripAdvisor users liked best. Several places in Spain are on the TripAdvisor list, which shows that Spain is a top place to visit and is safe to do so.

Pickpockets Barcelona

Most people who go to Barcelona have the most trouble with crime because of pickpockets.

Other crimes against tourists include stealing expensive watches worth between $20,000 and $100,000, but these are less common.

Tourists usually feel safe in Barcelona, but there are a lot of pickpockets and bag thieves in all of the areas with popular tourist sites.

Pickpockets are especially common on the pedestrian street Las Ramblas, near Sagrada Familia, in the central metro stops, and in the Sants train station.

Pickpockets don't usually bother people in other parts of the city unless they are near big tourist attractions.

Follow our safety tips for Barcelona to avoid being robbed by pickpockets.

These easy safety tips will help you stay safe in Barcelona and avoid being robbed or attacked by pickpockets.

Ten quick Barcelona safety tips

Important thief safety tips for Barcelona:

1. Don't put your wallet in your back pocket.
2. Don't leave phones and cameras on bar tables.
3. When you're in a busy area, wear your backpack on your front.
4. At cafes and coffee shops, keep your bags closed and on your lap.
5. Don't let people touch you or come up to you.
6. Don't play games like the three-shell game on the street.
7. Be especially careful on beaches and in cities.
8. Watch public shows with extra care.
9. Be especially careful on La Rambla, at the Sagrada Familia church, in the subway, and at Sants station.

10. Be extra careful in the hotel hallway, at airport bus stops, and on airport transportation.

And watch out if you're wearing an expensive watch. Gangs have sometimes gone after people who own very expensive watches.

Barcelona general crime

Pickpockets are the most common type of crime that tourists in certain parts of Barcelona have to worry about. Unfortunately, there can be a lot of pickpockets in touristy areas, so be careful in airports, train stops, the Metro, and your hotel lobby, as well as other places with a lot of people.

Most pickpockets in Barcelona don't hurt people. They try to take purses, cell phones, and wallets without the owner noticing. If you want to escape being robbed in Barcelona, you should read the safety tips below.

People who have lived in Barcelona for a long time, both from abroad and from Spain, will tell you that the city is usually very safe. When compared to countries in northern Europe, aggressive and dangerous behavior at night in Barcelona is very rare.

You don't have to worry about being in danger if you walk alone at night, and there are no serious crimes in the Barcelona metro. Day and night, you can often see cops on the streets and in traffic.

La Rambla, which is the street with the most pickpockets in Barcelona, usually has more police checks in the summer.

Both on La Rambla and in the Metro, the number of small crimes is going down. But watch out for thieves at the Sant stop. Since the Sants police station has been closed, there have been more people stealing bags at the station.

Most Spanish people don't drink too much, which makes the nightlife calm and reduces the number of fights and brawls.

People in Spain seem to smoke hash more than they drink too much, so you are more likely to be hugged than robbed.

Most muggings happen late at night, after 1:00 a.m., at the port end of La Rambla and in the lower part of the Raval neighborhood. As we've already said, violent muggings don't happen very often.

Most likely to be mugged are people who walk alone in those places very late at night and who might be a little drunk. Most of the time, anyone can walk the streets of Barcelona and ride the train without fear of getting hurt.

How to avoid being robbed in Barcelona

Pickpockets and small thefts do have a bad image in Barcelona, and they are very common in tourist areas.

Be careful in touristy areas like La Rambla, the Sagrada Familia temple, and anywhere near famous Barcelona sites.

You won't get robbed if you use common sense and take a few simple steps. Also, watch out when you're on or near tour buses in Barcelona, and be careful when you're riding the Metro.

Pickpockets don't bother people in other parts of Barcelona. We don't want to scare off tourists by sharing too many stories about specific robberies, but you should know that every day in Barcelona, many tourists have their phones and bags stolen.

Since the stories are always the same, there isn't much point in telling them again. We'd rather tell you what you can do to avoid being robbed in Barcelona.

If you follow the simple safety tips below, being robbed in Barcelona won't be part of your experience.

How to stay safe from pickpockets

1. Dress like you would in your own country

Try not to wear too much of a "tourist uniform" when you're on vacation. Just wear regular clothes and leave your old, colorful, hidden chest of holiday gear alone.

Old holiday clothes might be a little scary in terms of fashion, and looking too touristy makes you an easy target for thieves. We think that a good rule of thumb for what to wear is that if you wouldn't wear it at home, you shouldn't wear it on holiday.

Barcelona is mostly a casual clothes city, so just wear what you would normally wear at home, like a T-shirt and pants.

2. Dress for the weather.

The weather in Spain is not warm. Most of the time, shorts and short skirts are too cold to wear in the winter. During the summer, people usually wear light clothes. Barcelona clothes are mostly the same style as clothes in other European places, and they tend to change with the seasons.

3. Guidebooks and plans should be kept secret.

Don't look at maps until you need them. If you don't always have a guidebook and map in your hands, you'll look less like a tourist. So look at the map and then put it away.

When you want to check it again, go into a hallway or some other place where you won't be seen and pull out the map. We suggest a small, light guidebook or a plan of Barcelona that you can fold up. Hotels and places that help tourists can give you free maps.

4. Take care of your bag in the bars.

Don't hang your bag on a chair in a café or restaurant in Barcelona or leave it in an empty seat next to you or under the table. A thief could steal from you there. Keep a hand on your bag by putting it on your lap.

If it's under the chair or table, keep a hand on the strap if you can, but it's best to have it in your lap. If you look around, you'll see that most people in Barcelona keep their bags on their laps. We suggest that you buy a good, useful, anti-theft backpack with secret pockets and other safety features.

5. Don't show off your stuff.

Don't show the thieves in Barcelona what you have. Pickpockets like to steal from tourists who have nice things. If people see you as a "walking shop window," they may try to steal from you. The less you show, the less interesting you will be to thieves. We suggest that you keep your expensive phones and cameras in your bag or pocket when you're not using them. When you get to an interesting place in Barcelona, pull out your camera and take some pictures.

When you're done, don't just let the camera hang around your neck. Instead, put it away. If you have a big camera, you might want to get a neutral camera bag without a brand name on it. Or just cover or remove the labels. Don't show off an expensive camera with a zoom lens hanging off the side. Keep one hand on the lens and put it in your lap when you're sitting down. Don't show off a camera bag with the name of the brand on the bag and straps. Cover or take away the name of the brand. Bring fewer glasses.

When sitting, keep the camera bag on your lap. If you can help it, don't use a big bag. Put it in your lap. Never put it on the back of your chair or between your legs under the chair. Don't leave your phone or table on a bar table. Hide them when you're not using them. Do not place your money in the back pocket.

Leave your big wallet at home and just bring a small one with cash, two credit cards, and any I.D. you need. Don't leave the rucksack's zipper open, and don't carry it on your back with the top open. It's safer to wear it on your front or not to carry it at all.

6. *Don't set smartphones on tables.*

In Barcelona, don't put things like wallets, cell phones, or computers on tables in restaurants or cafes. Even more so outside and especially on La Rambla. Be careful if kids or homeless people try to sell you newspapers or magazines and say that the money will go to help the homeless.

If you forget something and leave it out in the open on a cafe table, these kids will come after you right away. Their trick is to put the paper on the table and act like they want you to look at it. Then, as they walk away, they quickly grab your phone or cash and put the paper back down. It's free, but it doesn't come cheap!

7. Don't bring watches that cost a lot.

People who own high-end watches should be careful. High-end watch names like Richard Mille, Patek Philippe, Hublot, Rolex, Hermes, Cartier, Panerai, Audemar Pigue, and Ulysse Nardin can be stolen by specialized gangs.

8. Put your pack on your front.

Backpacks and rucksacks should be worn on the front and kept closed with zippers. If you have a shoulder bag, put it under your arm and hold it with both hands. Make sure all of your bags are closed, zipped, and in your sight, especially when you are on the Metro.

Try to stay away from thin-strapped shoulder bags, money pouches, and camera straps. Pickpockets can cut through them quickly and take your bag without you even noticing. Don't put big wallets in your back pockets, and don't bring all of your cash and cards with you. Don't take it all with you. If you don't need to change money at a bank, leave your passport in the hotel safe.

9. *Nothing should get in the way.*

Be careful if anyone touches you, comes up to you, or does anything else strange. This could be a trick to get your attention off of them so they can steal from you. Scam artists often work in groups. While you are talking to or sidetracked by one, another is stealing from you. On the stairs is a common metro trick in Barcelona. Someone in front of you drops coins and keys on the stairs. It's a total mess, and while you're helping to pick up things, you're being stolen from behind.

So if you see or hear something strange, check your pockets and bags before helping other people. One more trick that pickpockets often use is to hug you and act like they are your friends. They might try this if you look tired or drunk late at night. So don't drink and hug! At the very least, don't hug people if you are drunk. You can also say that you have bird poop on your shoulder, and a "friendly person" will offer to help you brush it off. Again, it might get in the way. There are many different kinds of cons. So watch out for distractions, don't touch people, and push them away if you have to.

Pickpockets will rarely hurt you when they try to steal from you. If they think they've been caught, they just shrug their shoulders and move on to the next person. Be wary of offers of help, and if you take them, be very careful. Also, don't trust anyone who says they're from the cops and asks to see your I.D. Some thieves pretend to be cops and ask to see your I.D. They do this to try to steal your wallet.

Don't give your wallet to a stranger, and if someone says they are a police officer, ask them to take you to the police station.

10. Don't play street games.

Don't play games like the three-shell game on the street. Don't watch them at all. They are a con that is run by groups of thieves. You can lose your money playing the games, and because you're not paying attention, your pocket can also be picked.

The most common fake street game is the one with three bottle tops and a ball hidden under one of them. Or those three cards. This is a well-known street game called "trilo," which is played by "trileros." It is a total scam, and in 2011, Barcelona police made it a crime, so it isn't played as much anymore.

Four or five of the people watching the game and telling you to play are part of the "trilero" gang, and some of them might also be pickpockets. Watching street shows will confuse you, which makes it easier for pickpockets to steal from you.

11. Do not carry all of your credit cards.

Leave some cards where you live. Leave some cash and cards in the room safe of your Barcelona hotel or flat.

Remember that you don't need video cards, gym cards, library cards, and all the other reward cards you have at home in Barcelona. Take them out of your wallet before you leave the house. Or, get a safe wallet for trips. If your wallet gets stolen, at least you won't have to replace all of your reward cards at once.

Important tip: If your wallet is stolen and then returned to you with credit cards still in it but no cash, cancel the cards anyway. Basically, if you've lost your cards, you should cancel them. The person who gave you back your wallet might be part of a group of pickpockets, and they might have used a phone to take pictures of your credit cards so that they can be used online. So, if you lose your wallet, even for a short time, the best thing to do is to cancel all of your cards as soon as you can.

12. Advice on I.D. cards and papers

Today, you don't usually need a picture I.D. to buy smaller things with a credit card, but you will need it to change money at a bank, and you might need it if you want to buy something big.

But if you're just going out for the day and don't plan to spend a lot, leave your I.D. in the hotel safe or your room safe. Most good hotels have safes in the rooms.

Most hostels also have a safe or some other way to keep valuables safe at the front desk. And it's a good idea to bring extra copies of your passport and the phone numbers to call if you need to cancel your cards.

13. Keep money in a different place.

If your wallet or bag gets stolen, you will still have enough money for food and the bus ride back to your hotel in Barcelona. If you're in a relationship, don't put both of your wallets, phones, etc., in the same bag!

14. Write down important phone numbers

Write down a few familiar phone numbers and keep them in a place other than your wallet, or send them to yourself in an email. Some people have their phones stolen and then realize they can't remember any phone numbers. Don't forget that you can always get help by calling Barcelona's emergency numbers.

15. *Beach safety in Barcelona*

There are a lot of thieves on the beaches of Barcelona, especially near Barceloneta. If there are a lot of people at the beach, try not to bring anything valuable and keep it hidden. Don't close your eyes. Don't leave your stuff on the beach while you and the rest of your group go swimming. Be extra careful if the person next to you is alone and only has a towel, no books, sunblock, etc.

You won't know if you're sleeping, so don't doze off on the beach. Barceloneta is the worst beach for getting robbed. The others to the north aren't that bad. If you have time, go north of Barcelona to beaches that are nicer and where you won't be robbed. Also, you can trust the people who sell drinks on the beach. They often help catch and turn over pickpockets to the cops. You could use the old safety tip of putting your wallet in your shoe at the beach.

16. Safety in Barcelona metro

In the Barcelona metro, there are many groups of people who steal from people. Be aware of anything that might confuse you. People drop things or ask you questions. Check your things first, and then talk. We suggest that you carry a purse or bag with thick straps and a safe clasp. Always keep your pack in front of you. Keep the purse or bag close to your body, in front of you, or under your arm. When you are in the Barcelona metro, hold the bag tight at all times.

Putting your wallet in the front pocket of your trouser with your hand around it is the best place for it, never in the back pocket of your trouser. Also, watch out for cargo pants or shorts. The side pockets are useful and easy to get in and out of. Putting a thick rubber band around your wallet is a good idea. If you try to take your wallet out of your pocket, a rubber band will cause more friction and resistance than smooth leather. This increases the likelihood that you'll notice it slipping out of your pants.

Watch out for loud arguments or other commotions that could be set up to confuse you while someone else picks your pocket. If someone steals something from you, yell out right away to let other people know.

Don't be afraid of or feel bad about SHOUTING OUT! Tell the person driving the train or bus and yell for someone to call the cops. This makes it more likely that someone will pick up your wallet and run away. Ask the person who finds your wallet to wait until the cops arrive. This might be a partner! Often, a pickpocket's friend will try to find your wallet and give it back to you (without the money) to keep you from running after the pickpocket, who is his friend. If the Barcelona metro is busy or if someone bumps into you, be extra careful.

17. Don't drink too much

Most pickpocket scams work best when you've had too much to drink. Sorry to ruin the party for you.

18. Tell cops about a theft

Don't leave Barcelona until you've told the cops about a theft. If your wallet is found, there is a good chance that the money is gone, but maybe a kind Catalan will find it and give it to the cops. It could still have a lot of cards and pictures. And you can make a claim on your insurance with a police record.

At the time, you have to go to a police station (a comisara de Mossos d'Esquadra), but you can also report a theft from your hotel in Barcelona. Ask at the front desk. In the center of Barcelona, the police offices on Placa Catalunya and Nou de la Rambla are the easiest places to go to report a theft.

19. Watch out for fake cops

If you are stopped by police who aren't wearing uniforms, and they ask to see your cash, credit cards, or I.D., they might not be real police. Tell them you prefer going to the police station, but you don't want to give them your cash or credit cards. Real Spanish cops are not dishonest. Real police officers in Spain don't give tickets to people on the street.

Real Spanish police officers never ask tourists for their I.D. or to see their wallets or credit cards.

So, if someone in plain clothes stops you and wants to give you a ticket or see your I.D., they might not be real cops. Ask to see their I.D., be very careful, and tell them you'd rather go to the police station. Don't give them money or any kind of identification. They will take your money or wallet. Also, they might take pictures of your credit card numbers with their phones, so keep your wallet safe and, if they insist, get help in a store or office or look for cops in uniform.

Here are some updated emergency contacts for Barcelona:

National Emergency Number: **112** --- This is the general emergency number for all types of emergencies.

The *local police department*, Mossos d'Esquadra, can be reached at **088.**

Another contact number for *the city's police department* (Guardia Urbana): **092.**

The emergency number to contact *the fire department*: **080.**

There is a special emergency number for *medical situations*: **061.**

The American Red Cross is a nonprofit group that responds to disasters by providing aid to those in need by calling **934-268-282.**

The number to call to reach *the tourist office in Barcelona*, which can provide information and help in an emergency, is **(+34) 932 853 834.**

Please only call these numbers in the event of an actual emergency. Other lines and resources, such as police stations and hospitals, are accessible for less urgent matters.

Here are some numbers to call in case of an emergency in Barcelona, including those of the police and hospitals:

Local Police Stations:

Emergency Number: **_112_**

Mossos d'Esquadra (Catalan Police): **_+34 93 485 4400_**

Guardia Urbana (Local Police): **_+34 092_**

Hospitals:

Hospital Clínic: **_+34 93 227 5400_**

Hospital del Mar: **_+34 93 248 3000_**

Hospital de Sant Pau: **_+34 93 553 7575_**

Hospital Vall d'Hebron: **_+34 93 489 3000_**

Clinics:

CAP (Primary Care Centers): **_+34 93 227 9000_**

Barcelona Medical Center: **_+34 93 318 6205_**

Delfos Medical Center: **_+34 93 253 2121_**

Teknon Medical Center: **_+34 93 290 6200_**

Please keep in mind that these numbers and tools may change. If you need help right away, you should always call the emergency number for your area.

Over 100 common Spanish phrases with their translations

Here are over 100 common Spanish phrases with their English translations presented in a tabular form:

Spanish Phrase	English Translation
Hola	Hello
Adiós	Goodbye
Por favor	Please
Gracias	Thank you
De nada	You're welcome
Lo siento	I'm sorry
Salud	Bless you
Bienvenido/a	Welcome
¿Cómo estás?	How are you?
Estoy bien, gracias	I'm good, thank you
Mucho gusto	Nice to meet you
¿Cómo te llamas?	What's your name?
Me llamo...	My name is...
¿De dónde eres?	Where are you from?
Soy de...	I'm from...

Spanish Phrase	English Translation
¿Hablas español?	Do you speak Spanish?
Sí, hablo español	Yes, I speak Spanish
No hablo español	I don't speak Spanish
¿Dónde está el baño?	Where is the bathroom?
¿Cuánto cuesta?	How much does it cost?
¿Qué hora es?	What time is it?
Es la una	It's one o'clock
Son las dos	It's two o'clock
¿Puedo pagar con tarjeta?	Can I pay with a card?
¿Dónde puedo encontrar un restaurante bueno?	Where can I find a good restaurant?
Quiero un café con leche	I want a coffee with milk
La cuenta, por favor	The bill, please
¿Cuál es tu número de teléfono?	What's your phone number?
Tengo una reservación	I have a reservation

Spanish Phrase	English Translation
¿Dónde está la estación de tren?	Where is the train station?
¿Cuál es la contraseña de wifi?	What's the wifi password?
¿Qué me recomienda?	What do you recommend?
¿Dónde puedo encontrar un cajero automático?	Where can I find an ATM?
¿Qué significa...?	What does...mean?
Necesito ayuda	I need help
¿Puedes repetir, por favor?	Can you repeat, please?
Habla más despacio, por favor	Speak slower, please
¿Qué tal?	How's it going?
Estoy cansado/a	I'm tired
Estoy enfermo/a	I'm sick
Estoy perdido/a	I'm lost
No entiendo	I don't understand
¿Puedes explicar otra vez?	Can you explain again?

Spanish Phrase	English Translation
¿Puedo tomar una foto?	Can I take a photo?
¡Qué bien!	That's great!
¡Qué lástima!	What a shame!
¡Feliz cumpleaños!	Happy birthday!
¡Feliz Navidad!	Merry Christmas!
¡Feliz año nuevo!	Happy New Year!
¡Buena suerte!	Good luck!
¡Salud!	Cheers!
¡Que aproveche!	Enjoy your meal!
¡Hasta pronto!	See you soon!
¡Hasta luego!	See you later!
¡Nos vemos!	See you!
¡Adelante!	Come in!
¡Cuidado!	Be careful!
¡Ojo!	Watch out

Spanish Phrase	English Translation
Spanish	English
No puedo esperar más.	I can't wait any longer.
Lo siento mucho.	I'm very sorry.
Estoy ocupado ahora mismo.	I'm busy right now.
Tengo una pregunta.	I have a question.
No entiendo.	I don't understand.
¿Me puedes ayudar, por favor?	Can you help me, please?
No tengo idea.	I have no idea.
¿Qué significa esto?	What does this mean?
Me gusta mucho.	I like it a lot.
No me gusta.	I don't like it.
¿De dónde eres?	Where are you from?
Soy de España.	I'm from Spain.
¿Hablas inglés?	Do you speak English?
Sí, hablo inglés.	Yes, I speak English.

Spanish Phrase	English Translation
No, no hablo inglés.	No, I don't speak English.
¿Cuánto cuesta?	How much does it cost?
Está demasiado caro.	It's too expensive.
No puedo permitirme eso.	I can't afford that.
Me gustaría comprar esto.	I would like to buy this.
¿Aceptas tarjeta de crédito?	Do you accept credit card?
¿Dónde está el baño?	Where is the bathroom?
Necesito ayuda médica.	I need medical help.
¿Dónde puedo encontrar un cajero automático?	Where can I find an ATM?
¿Puedes darme indicaciones?	Can you give me directions?
Este es mi número de teléfono.	This is my phone number.
¿Qué hora es?	What time is it?
Son las cuatro y media.	It's four-thirty.

Spanish Phrase	English Translation
Es medianoche.	It's midnight.
Es mediodía.	It's noon.
Hace calor.	It's hot.
Hace frío.	It's cold.
Hace sol.	It's sunny.
Hay nubes.	It's cloudy.
Está lloviendo.	It's raining.
Hay nieve.	It's snowing.
El cielo está despejado.	The sky is clear.
Tengo hambre.	I'm hungry.
Tengo sed.	I'm thirsty.
¿Quieres salir a cenar?	Do you want to go out for dinner?
Estoy emocionado/a.	I'm excited.
Estoy preocupado/a.	I'm worried.
Estoy enfermo/a.	I'm sick.

Spanish Phrase	English Translation
Estoy aburrido/a.	I'm bored.

The book summary

The "Barcelona Travel Guide 2023" is the definitive guidebook for tourists who are visiting the city of Barcelona for the first time as well as seasonal tourists. This book presents an in-depth analysis of the city's top attractions, restaurants, accommodations, and activities.

The first section of the guide is an introduction to Barcelona, which covers its history as well as its culture. After then, it carries on to give passengers information that is useful in their day-to-day lives, such as the ideal times to visit, how to get around the city, and advice for maintaining their safety and health.

The guide is laid up in a neighborhood-by-neighborhood format, with each chapter devoting its attention to a different section of the city. Insider information from locals is provided in each chapter, along with a complete map, recommendations for sites, restaurants, activities, and more.

The guide not only discusses the most popular tourist destinations but also draws attention to some of the city's less well-known attractions, such as its local markets, street art, and hidden parks.

Seasonal advice is one of the things that distinguishes this book. The writers include recommendations for occasions and pursuits that can be experienced to their full potential during particular seasons, such as winter markets, summer festivals, and spring flower exhibitions, to name a few examples.

A section on day trips from Barcelona is also included in the guidebook. Within this part, readers will find suggestions for towns and sites located in close proximity to Barcelona that can be reached with ease using public transit.

Conclusion

To summarize, Barcelona is a great place to visit because there is something for everyone there.

In this lively and active city, there is always something new to find, so it does not matter if you've never been there before or you've been all over the world. Barcelona has everything you could want, from the breathtaking architecture to the delectable food and drink scene, from the beautiful beaches to the ancient landmarks.

We hope that you have found this travel guide to Barcelona to be both useful and helpful in preparing for your trip there. We have covered the most thrilling day trips that can be taken from the city, as well as the must-see sights, the greatest places to dine, and the best locations to shop. Additionally, we have included information that is useful in the areas of transportation, accommodations, and safety precautions.

Be sure to take things slow and immerse yourself in the culture of the area you're visiting. There is no shortage of once-in-a-lifetime experiences to be enjoyed in Barcelona, whether it be taking a leisurely stroll through the vibrant alleys of the Gothic Quarter, sipping sangria in one of the city's many attractive plazas, or taking a cable car ride to Tibidabo to watch the sunset.

Therefore, gather your belongings, make travel arrangements, and get ready to go on the experience of a lifetime in this breathtaking city. We hope you have a lovely trip and that this guide has helped to make your time spent in Barcelona an experience that you will always remember.

Appreciation

I'm grateful that you took the time to read my book. I hope you had a very good time and learned something from it. I would be forever appreciative if you could spend a moment leaving a positive review on the platform where you bought this book if you enjoyed it. Your encouragement means the world to me, your suggestion will guide me to improve more and your review may encourage other readers to find and read the book as well.

Thank you for your time and consideration.

Sincerely, Alexander J Collins

Reference

Barcelona | province, Spain | Britannica. (2023).

In *Encyclopædia Britannica*.

https://www.britannica.com/place/Barcelona-province-Spain

Barcelona 2023 - Barcelona pickpockets safety tips 2023. How to avoid pickpockets in Barcelona. (2023). Barcelonayellow.com;

https://www.barcelonayellow.com/bcn-tourist/115-safety-barcelona-top-tips-pickpockets

Printed in Great Britain
by Amazon